# Memories of a
# Preston Childhood

by

## ALAN WILDING

with a foreword by Tom Finney

Palatine Books, 1992

Memories of a Preston Childhood
by Alan Wilding

With a Foreword by Tom Finney and drawings by Isabella Walker

Published by Palatine Books, an imprint of Carnegie Publishing Ltd.,
18 Maynard Street, Preston PR2 2AL

Designed and set in New Baskerville by Carnegie Publishing Ltd.
Printed in the UK by The Bath Press, Bath

ISBN 1-874181-02-0

# Author's Note

Even if you didn't live in Preston there is much in this book that you may recognise in your own home town, particularly in Lancashire. My life as a lad was merely typical of many others, so I hope my story brings back happy memories of your own childhood. If it does then I'm glad to have shared mine with you.

*To Preston People*
*Past and Present*

# Contents

*Foreword, by Tom Finney* . . . . . . . . . . . . . . . . . vi

1   *Early Memories* . . . . . . . . . . . . . . . . . . . . . . 1

2   *Schooldays* . . . . . . . . . . . . . . . . . . . . . . 10

3   *Life as a Boy in Preston* . . . . . . . . . . . . . . . . 16

4   *Preston at War* . . . . . . . . . . . . . . . . . . . . . 38

5   *Working in Wartime* . . . . . . . . . . . . . . . . . . 48

6   *Preston Scientific Society and Preston Camera Club* . . 55

7   *Preston Lads in the Lake District* . . . . . . . . . . . 57

8   *Entertainment in Preston* . . . . . . . . . . . . . . . 60

9   *Social Attitudes* . . . . . . . . . . . . . . . . . . . . 69

10  *Evening Classes* . . . . . . . . . . . . . . . . . . . . 72

11  *Memories of Buildings, Markets and Shops in Preston* . . . 75

12  *Scouting in Preston* . . . . . . . . . . . . . . . . . . 85

13  *The Preston Guilds* . . . . . . . . . . . . . . . . . . 95

14  *Political Preston* . . . . . . . . . . . . . . . . . . . . 98

15  *Parks of Preston* . . . . . . . . . . . . . . . . . . . 100

16  *Sport in Preston* . . . . . . . . . . . . . . . . . . . 102

17  *Family Matters* . . . . . . . . . . . . . . . . . . . . 110

# Foreword

As a true and proud Prestonian, having lived a lifetime in the town, it brings nothing but pleasure to recall the days of childhood. Not for a single moment would I claim that life was easy or straight-forward in Lancashire during the '20s and '30s. Times were tough. There were six of us and we lost our mother when I was no more than a toddler.

Such a tragic loss obviously brings its own strain and problems, but, as with so many others, we were fortunate not only to have a strong family but also some tremendous assistance from neighbours and friends.

In the houses and streets of Holme Slack, which spread over a considerable area, we found unstinting assistance from adjoining families. Despite the hardships, mainly caused by a shortage of money, I remember being happy throughout my early years.

There was a real family atmosphere in those days and, happily, one of our neighbours was the author of this delightful new book, Alan Wilding!

Reading the text has brought the memories flooding back and I am sure many other 'locals' of our age bracket will find real treasures within the contents. Not only that, but I believe it will also provide more recent generations with a real insight into what life was like around 60 years ago. The names, the places, the events ... can it really all have been so long ago?

I am honoured to be asked to contribute in this small way, and I feel sure that *Memories of a Preston Childhood* will prove to be a valuable addition to the local bookshops. I also carries historical value and is an excellent read.

Tom Finney

## CHAPTER ONE

# Early Memories

W HEN I was born, in Preston Royal Infirmary in 1927, I was the youngest by ten minutes of four children, and we lived with my grandfather Thomas Wilding, a retired Headmaster, at 52 Hartington Road, off Strand Road, Preston.

My twin Marjorie and I were christened rather quickly in the hospital chapel, I was told, because we were so tiny that it was thought we might not survive. The two older children, Doreen and Norman, who were born five years earlier, were also twins. It was apparently so unusual to have twins at all in those days, let alone two sets, that my mother was given the help of a daily nurse from the Royal Infirmary; which says a lot for the community health care in Preston at that time. We all flourished as a result, and it soon became clear that we were outgrowing the house. So in 1931 we were allotted a council house at 29 Rose Lane, Holme Slack, where I lived for the next 20 years before I left the town, and I returned after that only to visit my parents until they died in 1969.

It is about my life in Preston as a boy and as a young man in those years before, during, and after the Second World War that this book is written.

My father, Harold Cooper Wilding, had moved to Preston, where he had many relatives, from Manchester, and had set up a duplicating ink manufacturing business in Owen Street, off Ribbleton Lane. My mother, Kathleen Mary Hoghton Cowell, a lovely young woman with raven black hair, was from Gamull Lane, Ribbleton, and worked as a demonstrator for the Singer Sewing Machine Company in Fishergate. She travelled round on her lady's tall bike with the basket in front, or in a light horse-drawn cart, to outlying farms and villages to show new purchasers how to operate their machines. They met during the First World War, in which my father served in the Border Regiment on the Somme and in Flanders, and was injured by gas warfare, and they mar-

1

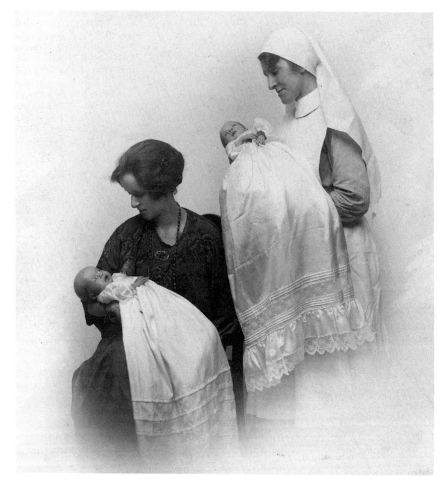

*Nurse Bright and Mother with her second set of twins.*

ried in 1920 in Christ Church, Bow Lane. Her first twins came along in 1922.

During my childhood Preston must have suffered to some extent from the 1930s depression, but because of its strong and broad industrial and commercial base, the effects didn't seem to show too much. It always seemed quite calm and untroubled to me. But perhaps it was due to our parents' success in shielding us from its worst effects that I don't recall too much hardship, though my father's income then was little more than thirty shillings, £1.50 a week.

In those days there were the great cotton mills of Horrockses and Hawkins, the big Victoria mill in Deepdale Mill Street, the Tulketh Mill,

2

*My mother was a lovely young woman with raven black hair.*

*My father served first in the Army Pay Corps and then in the Border Regiment in the First World War.*

and a dozen others. So though Preston's prosperity still depended largely on cotton, there were also the large electric tram manufacturing works of Dick-Kerrs (known by that name long after it became the English Electric Company), Goss's Printing Machines, Siemens Lamp Works, Thomas Drydens, and many others which gave work to thousands of men and women. The docks were very busy indeed, as were the railways, and both transported the products of the town to all parts of the country and of the world.

Preston already had a long and distinguished history, and its Guilds every 20 years had always been proud showcases of its industry, commerce, civic and religious traditions. The saying throughout Britain 'Once every Preston Guild' meant 'Once in a blue moon', it didn't happen very often but it was spectacular when it did!

Early in the 1930s an event took place in Preston that was to influence my whole career, from the time when I started my working life after leaving school in 1943 to when I left Preston in 1951, and for twenty five years after that. It was a visit by Sir Alan Cobham and his Flying Circus.

He brought his flimsy aeroplanes, most of them made of a wooden and steel framework covered by fabric, to a large field at the bottom of London Road, on the left by the river. There was also an autogyro, an early form of helicopter, driven forward by a propeller, so that the wind rather than an engine turned the rotors.

From the embankment above we had a grandstand view, and in spite of the much newer biplanes showing their paces, it was the older aeroplane in the show which caught my fancy. I'll never forget the sight, as a very small boy, as I watched in wonder that gossamer-like flying machine, so fragile yet so manoeuvrable, so noisy with its whirling propeller yet so graceful in its flight; and the thrill of seeing the pilot battling to keep control of it in the gusty wind. I decided then and there that I wanted to be part of them, I wanted to be with aeroplanes. For I had seen something of the

*I'll never forget the sight, as a very small boy, as I watched in wonder that gossamer-like flying machine.*

challenge and the sheer joy of flying.

It was an ambition I held to and which I was to achieve. For I subsequently played a part in the design of aircraft, in their manufacture, and later, in the Royal Air Force in being allowed to fly them too, as well as teaching how to maintain and look after them. On the wise advice of my father I resisted all offers to join other industries such as Leyland Motors, and kept to my original dream – a dream which started on that windy day near Walton-le-Dale.

For all its industry, my earliest memories of Preston were of a quiet leisurely place. Trams ground slowly, clanking, along Deepdale Road, struggling to climb the hill up to the Royal Garrison Hotel at the top, then turning left into Watling Street Road, so named I was told because part of the original Roman Watling Street passed beneath it. Not all the modern roads were tarmac'ed so they may not have been very different from those of ancient days, and with around fifteen years of peace after the First World War the town had settled down into a steady routine and calmness.

There were trams on all the principal roads of the town and routes went to all outlying areas. I think they were all double deckers, usually with 'bone-shaking' wooden slatted seats. The conductor would have to move the arm, which was in contact with the overhead cable, from one trailing position to the other as the tram reversed at the end of its route, and the driver moved to the cab at the other end. On some of them even the backs of the seats were pivoted to move across, so that the passengers could face forward as the tram started its return journey with that slow whine, going to a higher pitch as the motors took the load, and the clanking, as the tram went over the points at junctions. The tram tickets were little bits of coloured card from which the conductor would clip a hole or a little notch using a machine slung from his neck. If any of my readers want to re-create that scene almost exactly I suggest you try the National Tramway Museum at Crich near Matlock in Derbyshire; I did recently and had a ride on a tram and it all came back to me as if it were yesterday, it was great!

When tram lines were laid they were of course set level with the ground, so as not to obstruct other traffic, and at each side there was a

*Open top trams were used under the low bridge in Fylde Road.*
Courtesy Lancashire Library, Preston District

*A tram turning into Lancaster Road from Church Street, about 1934.*
Courtesy Lancashire Library Preston District.

channel to take the wheel flanges. My mother had a fine sense of the ridiculous and I remember, as a very small child, laughing at her story of the silly man whose bike wheels got stuck in the tram line channel, and he hadn't the sense to get off and lift it out, so he had to follow it all the way to the terminus in Deepdale Road! Usually, two sets of lines for trams going each way passed down the middle of each road, presumably to avoid the camber. So we had to walk out to the middle to board them; something that would be quite dangerous these days with so many cars. But cars were few and far between then, and anyway they were so noisy that you could hear them as well as see them a long way off. I must have been about seven years old when I was given my first ride on an 'omnibus' in Preston, but the buses didn't take over completely from trams until 15th December 1935, the last time a tram ran in Preston.

One of my happiest outings was always a visit to my maternal grandmother at her house 'Holyoake', 161 St. George's Road. She was Elizabeth, the widow of Walter Cowell who had been the Borough Lighting Superintendent. For many years after his death in 1924 she received a wonderful hamper of food, in an original wicker basket, from NALGO at Christmas and we would watch wide eyed as she opened it to reveal the goodies inside. Some time in the 1930s when the blue lamp over the entrance to Preston Police station in Earl Street was being converted from gas to electric, a note was found inside stating that the lamp had been made and installed by Walter Cowell, probably about 1900. I understand that the original lamp was transferred to the new police HQ in Lawson Street in 1972, so the note may still be inside it!

Because of the similarity of Granny's name to 'cowheels' which, with tripe and onions, were a delicacy in those days, our affectionate family name for her was 'Lizzie Tripe'! She was very nice and never failed to give us a penny or two for sweets when we visited her.

Her house was typical of many in that area in the early 1930s. Stone steps kept carefully 'sanded' using a block like a bar of soap, well polished brass door fittings and carpet edging, and a big front door with a black glass knob, and a patterned tiled porch. To the left inside was the parlour, always kept immaculate for visitors. Here were the velvet draped curtains, thick and nice to the touch, the deep pile carpet, the gleaming brass fireside implements and fender, and the china cabinet. We had to be good when we were in there. Yet I still think of that space between the sofa, which spanned the bay window, and those curtains, as my smuggler's den or my Aladdin's cave as I played there with my toys.

The living room next to it had gas mantle lighting, a wooden overhead clothes drying rack, and a cast iron firegrate with an oven beside it, always kept 'blackleaded' and shining. The oven had a heavy iron door with a latch, which made a noise when it was closed, and would be heated by the fire which could be stacked beneath and beside it. Cast iron bars across the front held a huge fire of coke or coal, and I would play on the big rug in front of it on winter nights, building Windsor Castle round towers out of dominoes. The bread which my Nan baked in that oven, I remember, had a taste all its own! Even her smoothing iron was cast iron, with little blocks which were heated in the fire then inserted into the iron. Her hair curling tongues would be heated similarly, and if they got too hot they would singe her hair and we could smell it. The big table was draped with a heavy blue velvet cloth when not in use and it would have a potted plant on top, probably an Aspidistra, in a polished brass container which sparkled in the firelight.

The kitchen had a stone sink and a stone flagged floor. Refrigerators were not known much in those days, but the stone shelves of the larder kept things very cool. Outside in the yard, at the far end was a toilet shed, a dampening experience in pouring rain, but worth it for the cosy sound of the rain on the corrugated iron roof when I was safe inside reading a comic. We were often in some danger of being lassoed on the way, however, by circular wooden rings, taken from butter or cheese casks in the Co-op next door, and thrown over the high wall for firewood for my granny. If we stayed overnight we might be wakened by the sound of a dog as its bark echoed weirdly down the alleyway between the backyards of the houses.

Upstairs lived a lodger called Horace Bolton, who used to play war games with hundreds of lead soldiers drawn up in battle array, which we were allowed to look at but not to touch. There were lancers, officers with drawn swords, Highland soldiers with rifles, even horse-drawn gun carriages, all about two inches high and brightly painted. There were guns, ammunition wagons and Standard bearers all a magnificent sight but not much fun if they didn't actually fight!

Straight opposite was St. Jude's church where I joined the Wolf Cub pack at the age of six, and my brother joined the Scouts because he wanted to play a kettle drum in the band. The Pack met in a small room underneath the church since their church hall wasn't built then, and I recall the solemn and impressive church parades on Remembrance Day when a bugler would come from Fulwood Barracks and play the Last Post. I was to return there thirty-six years later in equally sombre circumstances for the funeral of my mother, to the quiet dignity of her favourite hymn 'Abide with me'.

Another early memory connected with bugles, was the sound of the Last Post being played outside the guardroom at Fulwood barracks on Watling Street Road, where the Loyal North Lancs Regiment was housed. This plaintive, comforting sound would come drifting across Deepdale at 9 pm at my bedtime as if to say 'God is in his heaven and all's right with the world' as the bugler called an end to the day. It was a nice cosy way to settle down to sleep.

Across the corner from the church on the junction with St. Paul's Road was a shop called Craston's - a veritable box of sheer delight where I could find every kind of sweet, toy, and comic a boy could wish for, on which to spend my pocket money of one penny. Nearby was another shop, called 'Popinere and Byem', which sold sweets and cigarettes, and it was years before the penny dropped and I realised those were not the proprietors' names!

Even our fairly new Council house had only gas mantle lighting in some of its rooms when I was a boy. When that broke there was just a bare fan shaped flame until we could buy another mantle; it must have been quite a fire risk in a bedroom. Downstairs in the washroom there was a gas fired clothes boiler, and my mother would move the clothes around and press down on them with a thing we called a 'posser' which looked like an inverted copper colander with a long handle. There was a huge mangle with wooden rollers and a big curly-spoked cast iron wheel with a handle which I was allowed to turn, and it got the clothes really dry.

The streets of the town were still largely cobbled and gas-lit and a lamplighter would go round with a long pole with a hook and a light on the end. The hook would turn the gas tap on, and the light would ignite it, and I used to wonder why his light on the stick never blew out even in a wind! I suppose if I'd asked, he'd have told me.

Another man who still walked the streets of Preston carrying a long pole was the 'Knocker up'. In those parts where many workers lived who had to rise early for work in the mills for instance, he would tap on the upstairs bedroom window in the early hours to waken them. But as alarm clocks became available, or people ceased to live in such close communities, the system gradually died out.

Next door to us at number 31 Rose Lane, Holme Slack lived the Finneys for five years, one of whose sons was destined to be among the greatest footballers of all time, and to become a legend in his own lifetime. Further down Rose Lane lived Ben Fisher who later wrote for the *Lancashire Evening Post* under the name 'John Preston', and who, sadly, died in 1989.

## CHAPTER TWO

# Schooldays

A T FIRST we four children attended Deepdale Council School on the corner of St. Stephen's and Deepdale Roads. We had only slates within a wooden frame to write on with chalk or crayon, and when they were full we had to rub everything off, which meant we had no record of what we had learned. It was hardly satisfactory, and when my dad asked me what I had learned at school that day I couldn't show him, I had to try to remember. Miss Flannery, a friendly, comfortable smiling woman was my favourite teacher, and I hoped she could come with us when Marjorie and I were transferred to the newly built Holme Slack Council School, which opened on 31st May 1934, while the older twins went to Deepdale Modern School further down St. Stephen's Road. The Holme Slack school was only two hundred yards from home, and at the age of six we were drawn up into long lines, and allocated to the very first ever classes at that school. I got Miss Dickinson for my teacher and liked her very much though she didn't stand any nonsense. Every day we would be encouraged to drink milk from bottles that held ⅓ pint. If the weather was nice Miss Martin would let us have our 'playtime' on the sloping field behind the school, where we could roll about on the dry grass instead of running around on the tarmac playground at the front.

It was the Headmistress Miss Pritt, however, who seemed to have most influence on my time there. She was very fond of 'Singing Games', which I wasn't, because I thought they were cissy, and I tried very hard to sound like a crow with a sore throat at my audition. It was all to no avail however and I found myself in the team giving demonstrations around the area. But it was the innovation that followed that I preferred. This was a country dance team, dear to Miss Pritt's heart, and though Marjorie was in the team too it was apparently so obvious that I was head over heels in love, at the age of seven, with little Miss Jean Proctor of the

*The Singing Games and Country Dance team at Holme Slack School in 1934. I stood second from the right, back row, behind my twin, Marjorie, and was cross because Jean Proctor wasn't there.*

same age, that it was felt I should partner her. Jean's father was an optician in Church Street, but I had eyes only for his daughter!

The team went from strength to strength, and soon we were competing and winning at such places as the Lowther Gardens at Lytham, and at the Winter Gardens at Blackpool, against teams from all over the county. We wore the school colours, maroon and cream. The boys wore cream shirts and socks, a maroon tie with the school badge, and grey shorts. The girls wore cream blouses with a maroon neckerchief, maroon skirts and cream socks, and we all wore white plimsolls.

I felt very proud indeed as I led my partner and my team out onto the vast stage of the Winter Gardens Theatre, and stared across the footlights into the inky blackness of that vast auditorium. It was perhaps just as well that we couldn't see the audience because there really can't have been many, except the judges and a few proud parents. We won the competition and my twin and I were photographed for the local paper actually sharing a cream cake - a most unlikely event knowing us - and they even spelt our name wrongly too! Our speciality was a sword dance, during which we interlaced our wooden swords into a sort of linked trellis, rather like the Star of David, which we held proudly aloft at the end usually to much applause. There was also a nice little minuet called 'Touchstone', Miss Pritt's favourite. It was while we were dancing this

*Music from an already very ancient wind-up clockwork gramophone with a horn.*

once, on the lawn outside Penwortham Congregational Church, to music from an already very ancient wind-up clockwork gramophone with a horn that the motor ran down, and we danced slower and slower, and finally we all collapsed on the ground in helpless laughter!

Even though three or four of us were numbered among Miss Pritt's 'star pupils' academically, it didn't stop her ordering a caning when she thought we deserved it, and she shared her frowns and favours around in equal measure. She was a dear soul and just what that school needed for its first Head to get it off to a good start, and I have nothing but happy memories of my five years there.

In 1939 at the age of twelve I was very well qualified to go to Preston Grammar School. But it was decreed instead that I should go to Deepdale Modern School. This was not only because my elder brother and sister had been there, but also because it was considered to have a technical curriculum more appropriate to my avowed aim to be among aeroplanes, which had grown still firmer.

The more classical and somewhat commercial education of the Grammar School at that time, leading it is true, to University entrance, was not thought likely to meet my wish for a technical education and to enter Preston Technical College. The course I took was to lead to a Masters Degree, anyway, though in a more roundabout route. So I didn't feel any regrets at the course of my career, and the Deepdale Modern School delivered all that I could have asked of it.

Its Head was a tall, greying man called Mr Wilson whose one stern glance over those pince-nez glasses would have struck fear into Samson! But he was always fair and a tower of strength to any student with a problem. It was a mixed school, but for practical training the boys would use the woodwork and 'technical' workshops at the western side of the left quadrangle, while the girls would use the eastern side of the right quadrangle for their cookery and domestic studies. The assembly hall was in the middle and we would hear virtually the same prayers every morning at assembly, so that any one of us could recite them backwards in our sleep! - 'It is very meet, right, and our bounden duty ...' But it was a happy place even if a teacher did catch me once climbing over the back

12

fence when I was late in, trying to avoid the 'prefect picket' at the main entrance!

Our teacher, John Bagot, the source of that early technical education in mechanical theory, science, technical drawing and maths, also taught English Literature rather well. He would delight us with the humour and beauty of the English language one day, and scare us out of our wits by reading Edgar Allan Poe to us the next. There was another teacher, Mr Williams whom we called 'Itchy' for his habit of scratching his nose. There was a Miss Ward, and there was Mr Jones, a benevolent man, who also taught maths and science, whom we rather unkindly called 'Bonzo' because he had a certain resemblance to a bulldog. But then so did Winston Churchill and he was proud of it! Our woodwork teacher was the able Mr Duckworth who was always known as 'Benny'. He was a fierce disciplinarian, he had to be with a class of unruly lads using sharp woodcutting tools; but he could make a dovetail joint in satin walnut that would make you marvel at its perfection. His cry of 'Stand by your benches!' at the start and end of each lesson, produced as quick a response as any army sergeant ever achieved in a barracks!

Our art teacher was Vincent Newton, who once invited our whole class to his lovely home near Garstang where he gave us all fruit from his orchard. He also taught Civics, all about local government and institutions, English, history, and an unusual subject 'Gardening Science'. Quite recently, when I was attending a rather boring committee meeting, while things were being discussed that didn't concern me, I found myself doodling and suddenly realised that the pastoral scene I was sketching was one that 'Vinny' had taught us to draw all those years ago!

There was also Miss Pearson, a hardworking lady who stood for no slacking in her pupils, and could teach English, singing, and history, as well as French. But this versatility was not unusual, most of the teachers were very clever and could teach lots of things, and they might teach one subject to one form and something quite different to another.

There was Miss Kirkham, a tall young lady who also taught English; Mr Hemmingway, First form teacher for 1B; and a tall powerful red haired man whom we called 'Taffy' Baron who would say something then frown and ask 'Ave you 'eard that Boy?', but he was friendly enough once you got to know him, and was just trying to keep our attention.

Though in company with my friends and rivals Arthur Bennell and Geoff Halsall I seemed to do quite well in most topics, seeming to rotate the top places between us, I never really understood Miss N. Aspinall's French, though I'm told her accent was impeccable. Better perhaps than our pronunciation of her name! I just wasn't good at French, and that was that, though she was an able teacher. So it was a triumph of will when I got as much as 7% for French once, and I would have been a good prototype for that English agent who acted as a French policeman in the *Allo allo* TV series!

The school colours were brown and white, so the boys wore a brown blazer with the school badge of an open book on the breast pocket, the school tie with a metal badge, grey shorts and socks to match. It was quite usual then to wear shorts right up to the final year at the age of fourteen or fifteen, and of course we didn't mind or think we were too grown up for that as long as everyone else was the same. It was just the standard wear then, which was thought to give more mobility to lads running around. These days many a kid is in long trousers by the age of seven or so, which probably gives better protection against scuffed knees, the sun and the weather.

The girls wore brown gymslips with a brown hat with the same school badge on it, and used to play a lot of netball. They were very good to watch, and though we'd jeer a bit at times we were quite proud of them really, because they were very successful and gave the school a good name.

The school was divided into 'Houses', Saxons, Angles, Danes and Normans, named of course after successive invaders of Britain. I was a Norman, as predictably my elder brother had been. But I didn't want to be, because I thought they had been horrible to Robin Hood and the Saxons, so I wanted to wear the red colour of the Saxon House. And anyway they had a better football team.

Miss Clitheroe, our geography and history teacher was a favourite with us all. Instead of boring us with too many details of far away places we were unlikely to need to know about, she concentrated on our local geography. She taught us about the towns and villages about us, their history, their industries, their people, how the hills and valleys were formed; and in particular how the Lakes had been created by glaciers mostly radiating from the central massive of Scaefell. It was partly a wish to stand on those mountains and see for ourselves that was the reason for many youth hostelling and fell-walking holidays which I and my school friends took later, and for the development of a love of the Lake District which I have to this day. To think it all started with the teachings of that interesting and enlightened Geographer. Those were good lessons, and it showed in our results. What a very good school that was!

If my friends called me a bit of a 'swot' at times, it was partly because I found the subjects so interesting, and the teachers seemed to have motivated me quite well in spite of my being innately lazy, and surely that's what they were there for! Success didn't come easily to me, I had to work hard. But actually there was a second reason. I'd noticed I was getting out of breath rather easily, and at the age of 11 I was diagnosed as having a faulty heart valve, and told that I mustn't even walk quickly, let alone run.

This went on for almost four years, all of the time I was at Deepdale Modern, and was a bit of a nuisance, because I wasn't even allowed out to the school playground. So since I was confined inside each breaktime there seemed little else to do but read things. It wasn't the sort of thing you talk about much so I just told people I preferred to stay in, though the teachers knew. It cleared up by about the

*'Flowers scattered in all directions'*

time I was sixteen and then I had a lot of running about and sport to catch up on. In fact, if I remember rightly our perceptive Dr Lytton, whose surgery was at the top of St. Paul's Road, actually recommended hill walking to build up my stamina again, to get plenty of fresh air and exercise; which was handy because it was what I was determined to do anyway.

Near to the school was Smith's shop where you could buy delicious Tiger nuts. It was our Tuck Shop and at least was something of a solace for me, unable to play out, or for those who, like a popular school chum of ours, Barbara 'Babs' Holden, had seen their father go off to the War and had found a quiet corner in the school to cry.

Travelling to school daily from Holme Slack was not without its slight hazards. Preston had a large Catholic population at that time and at lunchtimes, most of the local Catholic children seemed to travel up St. Gregory's Road in the opposite direction to us Protestants, making St. Patrick's Day rather interesting. While we had to endure the jeers and taunts on that particular day, there was generally no problem; it was purely traditional and never came to blows, and I had good friends of both religions.

However, my twin nearly 'blotted her copy book' once. She went everywhere on roller skates at one time; and when as a small girl she went with a little Catholic friend of hers to St. Gregory's church to deliver some flowers for the altar, it never occurred to either of them that it might not be appropriate to enter the House of God on roller skates. So down the aisle they went at some speed, her friend leading. Suddenly her friend remembered her manners, and stopped dead to curtsey and to genuflect. Marjorie, quite unable to stop went clean over her and both finished up in front of the altar, spread-eagled like novice nuns, with flowers scattered in all directions! But the wrath of Heaven didn't descend on her on that occasion - after all He was a child Himself once!

## CHAPTER THREE

# Life as a Boy in Preston

IN THOSE 1930s years before my teens, life was great fun in Preston. But we had to make it so by making our own amusements. Television hadn't reached the town, so we needed a well developed sense of 'let's pretend' and a fertile imagination. There was an area North East of Fulwood barracks between Watling Street Road and Fulwood Hall Lane which curved round to run parallel to it. In this small area, which we called the 'Hills and Hollows', where the Battle of Preston was said to have been fought in 1648 during the Civil War, we would play quite happily for hours. One time the hills would be sun-baked desert dunes and we would be the French Foreign Legion tramping the hollows looking for fierce Tuareg Arabs; another time we would be a platoon of the Loyal North Lancs. descending from the hills, all four of us, to wipe out a whole German Army regiment.

Sometimes we would go beyond there further North down Fernyhalgh Lane to Squire Anderton's Wood. Now there was a playground for boys! There was a stream running through it, parallel to a parkland track which led to a gracious house at the far end beyond a wooden bridge. We would climb the trees, ford the stream, we even built a rope bridge across it once and one of my friends fell off it into the water. There were bluebells in the wood, birdsongs of every description, and it was a most delightful parkland playground where no-one bothered you as long as you didn't actually light fires. Very near to where I live in Scotland now is just such a lane, and I seldom go down it these days without thinking of the fun we had so long ago.

Once, when I took our old dog Bess to Squire Anderton's Wood, we called in at the Lady's Holy Well in Fernyhalgh Lane to pay our respects at the shrine to the Virgin Mary. But Bess slipped on the wet surround and fell in and came out holier than any of us. But she was very generous

*Squire Anderton's Wood.*

*Our old dog, Bess, fell into the Ladywell at Fernyhalgh.*
Photo reproduced by kind permission of the *Lancashire Evening Post.*

about it, and shared her sanctity around when she shook herself, and we all got a bit; though a nun who happened to be there wasn't very pleased! But it was an accident and I'm sure Forgiveness isn't confined to humans.

We used to play down by the brook in the 'Deepdale' from which the area got its name. We reached it by a track at the end of Manor House Lane at Holme Slack and the track led up to what we called 'Uncle Tom's Cabin' on Watling Street Road, near Highfield Avenue. There had been an old shack there at some time, and though it was long gone the name had stuck. That part and along to the west was called 'Happy Valley' - a good name because we had lots of fun there. By the brook was a stunted tree which had a branch that overhung the water, and we would tie a rope to the branch and play 'Tarzan' as we swung over, occasionally not quite making it and hanging on over the water until someone pulled us back. Heaven knows what pollution went into that brook, for we frequently came away with sore throats, and our mothers would beg us not to play there, fearing typhoid. But it was too much of an attraction to heed their warnings, I'm afraid, and countless times toy ships made out of paper would set out on perilous journeys to foreign lands from near that foot-bridge over the brook, or would get stuck, go soggy, and sink before they were even out of sight.

My particular chums at that time were Bernard Mace and Roland Boyes, together with the Yates brothers Peter, Jack and Ron, Dennis Trott, Raymond Bowman, and Colin Pimbley. It was nice to hear from the Yates's recently, but I wonder what happened to all the others? It's such a pity when you lose touch with old friends. We used to roller-skate together and once I was knocked down by a large lad on a bike, who was charging along at great speed. I hit my head on the curb, was concussed, and had to stay off school in a darkened room for several weeks.

I was nearly the cause of Roland Boyes being asphyxiated on one occasion, when we were holding a Bonfire Night party in his back garden. The fireworks were in a box on a bench across a corner between two walls; and for some reason, Roland was standing in the triangle thus formed, when I came too near with a sparkler, and the sparks fell into the box and ignited the whole lot. Sheer hell broke loose, whizzbangs, rockets shooting off horizontally, screeches, hisses, Roman Candles sending up coloured fountains, deafening reports, thuds, bangs – and Roland was trapped there! Fortunately, some brave person went straight into the inferno, risking everything, grabbed him and yanked him out of it, coughing and spluttering from the smoke, and his mother had to revive him with 'smelling salts'. Fortunately and much to my relief he soon recovered.

If we wanted to go to Ribbleton from Holme Slack we would go via the 'Forty Steps' by a track which led from the end of Holme Slack Lane. There was a stile and the steps led down to the Longridge railway line and up the other side. But there weren't forty of them and I never quite knew why they were called that, unless some had got buried out of sight. Trains would occasionally go along the line and I think Croft's brickworks had its own siding, so we had to keep a look out and skip across quickly, which added a bit of extra excitement to our visits to the Carlton Cinema at Ribbleton.

To the right of the track to the forty steps were large sand pits belonging to Croft's. We would stand on the brink of the quarried holes and jump down several feet into soft sand. Once I landed awkwardly and winded myself so much I thought I'd never get my breath back and would die; but Geoff Halsall forced my head down between my knees and I soon recovered. I don't know where he learned that trick but it worked! I think if I and my friends had listed all the things our parents hoped we wouldn't do, it would exactly match all the things we did! So life around Holme Slack was not without its excitements in those far off days!

I suppose on the credit side I could show the fact that I and several of my friends were members of St. Oswald's church choir at Deepdale. It was I think an oasis of peace and tranquillity in a busy childhood world, and I was acutely conscious of the timelessness and beauty of the

18

church liturgy; though even there I kept getting ticked off by the Elders for one misdemeanour or other, not least for singing less than reverential words to some hymns, and for playing the paper game 'hangman' with my friends during the sermon: 'Noughts and crosses, perhaps, if you are bored,' they said, 'but certainly not hangman!' The stiff Eton collars we wore looked like cone shaped white volcanoes with our heads sticking out of the crater, and would rub our necks and make them sore on hot sticky summer Sundays. But I liked the services really, the Communion, Matins and Evensong particularly the Te Deum, the Nunc Dimittis and the Magnificat, (one of my choir friends called his feline pet 'Magnifi'), and I would go three times a day most Sundays. There was a very good organ from which beautiful sounds, sometimes quiet and gentle and at other times loud and stirring would come, with the console mounted on top of the Rood screen separating the chancel from the nave.

So in spite of being anything but an angel in a cassock and surplice, I had a genuine regard for the place and its atmosphere, and I was thus a willing candidate for Confirmation when the time came in 1942. However, it turned out to be something of a disaster. For one thing they only sent a suffragan bishop, when I felt that for such an occasion no-one less than Canterbury or York would do; then some idiot had me sitting next to a chap who was very tall indeed for his age, while I was still but knee high to a grasshopper. So when we knelt at the Bishop's chair and he put a hand on each of our heads to bless us, one hand was high up, and the other so low down on mine that a titter ran through the congregation, which made me squirm with embarrassment, and brought a stern reproving glance from the bishop.

However, his text for his sermon 'Fear not, for I am with thee' stuck in my mind; and was to be a help many years later, when I was being allowed to fly a Jet Provost aircraft over Norwich, under the guidance of a regular pilot. I taught Theory of Flight and felt that a little practice would not go amiss. Since I was showing interest in the Cathedral, my colleague suggested I bank round and circle it to have a good look. But I rather over-did it and banked so steeply, at almost 90 degrees in fact, and at such a slow speed that the aircraft began to side-slip alarmingly downward, and the pilot had to take control rather quickly, for it was a situation I wasn't used to; theory hadn't prepared me for the real thing. As he struggled to bring the plane level, those words came back to me: 'Fear not, for I am with thee'.

Every Easter, as children, along with thousands of other Prestonians we would go 'Pace egging' on Avenham Park. On the Monday, we would arrive early at the slope, just below the Summer House at the end of Avenham Walk near the tall flag pole. There we would roll our painted hard boiled eggs, the funnier the face drawn on them the better, usually

*Every Easter we would go 'pace egging' on Avenham Park on the slope below the tall flag pole.* Photo courtesy of *Lancashire Evening Post.*

of Daddy because he would join in the fun and pull a funny face while we drew it. We would roll chocolate eggs and oranges too; the band would play in the bandstand in the middle and the whole valley of the park would be a sea of excited happy children and their families. People were very gregarious in those days, especially on public holiday events like that, and would enjoy those simple pleasures together.

Christmas when I was a lad in Preston had a special magic. The town would be gaily decorated, and there was an enormous illuminated Christmas tree on top of the cigarette kiosk in the centre of the crossing in the Miller Arcade. Marjorie and I would ask each other what we wanted for Christmas, and each would spend exactly the same amount. On one occasion we decided we would each like a camera which they sold at Woolworths in Fishergate. In those days the store had a sign which claimed there was 'nothing over sixpence' (2½p), and generally there wasn't. But a camera that worked, even if the body was only plastic, was more than they could offer at that price. So they sold the front half on one stall for 6d. and the back half on the next one for another sixpence! And they made sure you didn't go away with just one part. We each bought a camera then solemnly handed it over to each other, because that was the ritual we often followed as twins. But of course we didn't know about our other presents. So a few days before Christmas we

20

would wait till the fire was out, then shout up the chimney to Father Christmas to tell him what we wanted. We couldn't always understand why, because we'd probably already told him in Merigold's or Mear's shop in Fishergate that afternoon. We would decorate the house with streamers we had made at school, and make others, sticking them together with flour and water because it was cheaper than glue. Bess our dog would have tinsel wrapped round her collar and we would have a small Christmas tree with a silver star on top.

On the morning of the Great Day my parents would line us all up in the hall outside the living room door, youngest first, oldest last. I was forever grateful for that ten minutes age difference between me and Marjorie, because it meant I was allowed to open my presents first. Norman was three quarters of an hour younger than his twin so it was Gents before Ladies in our house at Christmas. With our eyes tightly shut, no peeping allowed, we were led to our place round the big table where, fastened to a table cloth and hanging down each side, were not just Christmas stockings but Pillowcases absolutely bulging with presents of all shapes and sizes! Our parents were very good indeed to us at Christmas and would save up for months ahead, depriving themselves to do so, because we were not well off.

Everyone had to watch while I opened mine, then Marjorie hers, and so on. It must have been very frustrating for Dad who came last! Bess had her presents too, and there was an atmosphere of special magic and excitement with a sort of glow over everything that made that day quite unlike any other. At Christmas I always understood why Peter Pan didn't want to grow up!

We usually had a goose rather than a turkey because we felt there was more taste to it; and my mother would carry in the cooked bird proudly and ceremoniously on an enormous blue patterned plate, that had been in the family for years and years (and which I still have); and she would save the dripping and rub it on our chests if we had winter colds. After a lovely lunch, for she was an excellent cook, we would go out to play and meet our friends and show each other our presents and play with them, just like kids do now. When we came back for tea it would be made on that one day in the year in a special pewter-coloured teapot that had once belonged to Joseph Livesey the founder of Teetotalism. We maintained all these family traditions a generation later when my own sons were young, and they assure me they will continue them in their turn as far as possible. Such family traditions are important.

In winter my mother would always keep a large pan of home made broth simmering on the hob of the living room fire. It was made with fresh vegetables, lentils, pearl barley and lots of meat stock, and it used to warm us 'right down to the insides of our big toes' as we used to say. Another favourite was 'A dish of potatoes with sausage on top' rather

*My Great Grandfather, John Hoghton, made and sold prams at 113 Church Street.*

*An advertisement for my Great Grandfather's pram shop next to the Bluebell Inn on Church Street.*

like hot pot, with slices of potato and some onion, baked in a dish with milk or water; but when they were nearly cooked the top would have a layer of sausages baked on it, and it was delicious! Doreen would come home from her school cookery lesson with an enormous Lancashire hot pot, which she'd made complete with crisp pastry crust, which had cost just sixpence for the materials (2½p today) and my mother would warm it up again and it would feed all six of us.

When there was ice on the footpaths we would make slides, and it was then that the kids who wore clogs had the advantage, because they had metal runners on the soles and could slide further. I was quite envious of those who had them. Clogs were a wonderfully practical shoe for hard wear, though they were perhaps rather heavy for a young foot. They were made of thick leather with metal edging and a kid would grow out of them long before they wore out. The clogs would then be passed on to the next in the family. Unfortunately there was a lot of silly snobbishness about wearing shoes in preference, when in fact the old Lancashire clog saved many families a fortune in footwear.

Both our parents were virtually 'only children' - my mother had a younger brother but he had died at the age of nine, so we had no uncles or aunts of our own, only those of our parents, which made them Great uncles and aunts to us.

My mother's mother, Granny, of St. George's Road, was one of nine sisters, not untypical in her Victorian generation. Each was given a second name to mark her position in the family. There was Emily Septima the seventh daughter, Ada Octavia, the eighth, Maud Nina, the ninth, and so on. Granny Elizabeth was I think the fifth child. Their father, a man called John Hoghton, a very aristocratic-looking man with a beard, had owned a pram shop at 113 Church Street next to the Bluebell Inn. The prams, bath chairs and invalid carriages were assembled and upholstered on the premises, and in further accommodation he acquired in Bluebell Yard. My granny was actually born in the Bluebell Inn when I believe her mother suddenly went into labour, and that was the nearest accommodation available, and she got her leg pulled ever after for having been born in a pub! Since her father had no son his daughters ran his business when he died, and very well by all accounts.

Three of them, Emily and Margaret lived in some style with their husbands and with Ada, a widow, in a big elegant house at number 8 Sunnybank Terrace, Grimsargh, which formed the northern end of the terrace. They had moved there in 1932 from a fine house at number 82 Stephenson Terrace on Deepdale Road. It is surprising how clear one's memory can be of events at the age of five or less, because I can still conjure up a clear vision of visiting them at Stephenson Terrace, and seeing the same sort of grandeur of ornate plastered ceiling roses and cornices, potted plants, tasselled rugs and gentle elegance that my granny, their sister, had at St. George's Road.

My Great Uncle Herbert Blacow, Emily's husband, was a well known and much respected funeral director whose parlour was at 1 Garstang Road, Preston. His hearse was pulled by jet black horses with purple plumes on their heads - he liked 'to do things properly' and got most of the 'big' funerals of prominent people in the town. When boiled ham was an expensive luxury, and the mourners were offered it at the meal following the funeral, then it had been a good and proper funeral, well managed, for the deceased had been 'Buried with ham'. It was, in other words, 'A gradely do'! But even in that profession it was possible to see some humour, and Uncle Bert used to tell the story of the sexton who approached a very old man attending a funeral and asked 'Eeh Grandad, 'ow old are ta?', 'I'm ninety fower' came the answer, 'By Gum!' said the sexton 'It's 'ardly worth thee goin' whoam!'

My Great Aunts' and Uncles' house, at Sunnybank Terrace Grimsargh, had two grandfather clocks and a smaller 'grandmother' clock, a highly polished piano, chintz curtains and sofa, a beautiful mahogany table and willow patterned plate crockery. Great Uncle Bert was not only a pigeon fancier of some note, with a fine pigeon loft and summer

*Great Uncle Herbert Blacow's funeral parlour was at no. 1, Garstang Road, and his hearse was driven by Mr. Harris and pulled by jet black horses.*
Courtesy Dorothy Blacow Satterthwaite.

house at the end of his large garden, he also grew the most perfect roses, and would honour me by cutting one of his best for my button hole as I left after a visit. He and our Great Aunts once took us four children on a ride on a small train whose engine was called 'Little Annie', which plied between Grimsargh and Whittingham, and it was the very first train ride I ever had.

His wife Emily made dresses in a little hut behind the house, warmed in winter by a tall paraffin heater which created a lovely cosy feeling when the warmth hit you as you entered. I used to love going to Grimsargh, it was nice just to be there for it was so peaceful. But all things come to an end, and Aunty Maggie, Mrs Atkinson, suffered a leg amputation at the age of 83 and died soon afterwards. Dear Aunt Emily died, and Uncle Bert died tragically just outside his own house, a great loss to Preston. The last and youngest remaining aunt, Ada, Mrs Martin, came to live with us and lived to the ripe old age of 92, and she and I would chat in front of the fire as she told me tales of Preston long ago. Herbert Blacow's daughter Dorothy was a most vivacious young lady and great fun to know. I still receive lively letters and enjoyable phone calls from her in Bournemouth over 50 years later, my last link with that remarkable and interesting family.

When I was a small boy I knew that if either my Granny or one of those imposing Great Aunts came to town, we would be taken to Booth's cafe for morning coffee or afternoon tea. Now Booths still had the style and atmosphere of more elegant times. Downstairs was a delicatessen which sold such things as specialist teas and spiced ginger. But when you entered by the western door and climbed the stairs to the restaurant there was a small platform at the turn of the stair. There a trio or a quartet would play selections from 'The Merry Widow' or 'The Desert Song' to the sound of polite conversation, the tinkle of tea cups and the crunching of toasted teacakes, as waitresses in spotless white

*Great Aunt Alice and Uncle David Morphy of Slynedales – 'that charming and gracious lady and her kindly husband'.*

aprons and headbands like tiaras plied between the tables. But as I entered my teens I preferred to go to the Kardomah further down Fishergate where I could fidget as much as I wanted!

If I haven't any personal memories of my other grandmother, my father's mother, Annie, née Cooper, it was because she died in 1920 before I was born. But her gentle influence was to pervade much of our early life through the example she set, and through the tales, which both our parents told, of her kindly, genial nature. She was one of ten children from a Preston family, the Coopers, whose branches included the Margerisons, the soap people, (in fact three of them married Margerisons so the family links became quite strong); Turners the coal merchants were another branch, and there was quite a well known writer Alfred Benjamin Cooper who wrote romantic Victorian novels, and from whom I may have inherited my own love of writing. All who knew Annie Cooper Wilding said she was quite the kindest most loving person they had ever known. Another of her sisters, Alice, had married David Morphy, a woollen merchant; and I remember being taken to visit this elegant and charming lady, my last surviving paternal Great Aunt, in their fine big house called Slynedales at Slyne, near Lancaster, and going up a curving drive through a lovely garden to be met at the door by a butler, no less, and having our coats taken by a housemaid! When dinner was announced my Great Uncle David, a kindly man who understood children and made us feel quite at home, took his place at the head of the table and carved a huge roast. Such memories of the last of those days of charm and elegance made a lasting impression on me.

My paternal grandfather, Thomas Wilding, Annie's husband, came to live with us at Rose Lane, and I remember as a small boy that he gave me a special crayon pencil which was red at one end and blue at the other. He was a very erudite man with a marvellous way with words, as could

*The Hornby train was another source of endless pleasure.*

be seen from the letters he wrote to my father in the mud of the Flanders trenches. His words must have been of great comfort at those times. The fact that he was a headmaster may also explain why I have so much enjoyed thirty-three years of teaching; perhaps it was in my blood. How sad it is to think, though, that apart from that worthwhile inheritance, my only memory of his whole life is the fact that he gave his grandson a pencil! He died when I was about five.

One memorable Christmas my brother decided that the time had come for him to hand over to me his extensive Meccano and Hornby train set, which he had collected over many years. The Meccano set consisted of steel strips and plates, angle irons and brackets, all punched with holes at intervals. There were wheels, clockwork and electric motors, rods, spring clips, nuts and bolts; all able to be assembled into great towers from floor to table with an elevator lift inside. Cranes like derricks could sweep out over a wide area and pick up quite heavy things. Aeroplanes could be built that didn't look much like the real thing but with a bit of imagination would become the big giant Handley Page Hannibal and Argosy aircrafts that were then flying for Imperial Airways out of Croydon. I believe my later interest in aircraft construction stemmed from those toys which would keep me quiet for hours. The Hornby train set was another source of endless pleasure. I could now design my own railway layouts with the train passing over or under bridges, with all manner of accessories like points, coaches, engines, trackside equipment, station buildings and even a model chocolate dispenser. So if my parents' slippers went missing from their bedroom it was probably because they were being transported as goods freight to some station beyond the bathroom on the six-fifteen express!

In fact apart from our roller skates, those were about the only bought toys we had. If we wanted anything else we had to make them. The skates were pressed into service to make skate boards, which we sat on - not stood on as they do today - and I nearly lost my life when a van shot across my bows as I was descending at speed down Rose Lane Hill. But I hardly expected it because any kind of vehicle was so rarely seen in those days. Later we made trolleys using pram wheels, and these could be steered, and we fitted crude brakes to them so they were much safer. But again I nearly suffered an early demise when I picked up a very strange object while searching for pram wheels on a nearby rubbish dump, as I shall recount later.

Most of my friends and I made our own gadgets, it gave us something to do in the evenings, and the photographic enlarger I made when I was rather older is still giving good service 50 years later, though I've had to convert it for colour printing recently. The enlarger easel, safe light, and print drier/glazer made out of a reversed reflector from an electric heater, still all work well. I believe it was more satisfying doing things like that for ourselves than saving up to buy things. Of course we had 'Tops and whips' too and marbles. We made pairs of stilts, and I was just saying to Fred Lang 'Hey look! – I'm getting quite good at this!' when I fell off – 'Getting quite good at what?' he asked. We played 'Conkers' with chestnuts which we hardened in the oven in autumn, and sometimes we would condescend to play Hopscotch with the girls for it was generally thought to be more of a girls' game. Rolling hoops was quite popular. The proper way was to buy a hoop of steel rod, and a handle would be supplied with a loop round the rod so that it was always in contact, you couldn't lose it, and you just had to pull or push this and the friction would start the hoop rolling. But that seemed a bit too easy for us, so we used to get an old car tyre and a thick stick and give the tyre a good whack with it to start it rolling, then chase after it and give it another and so on. Mine nearly knocked over an old lady as it got ahead of me down Rose Lane Hill and she wasn't very pleased. We had Yo-yos, slid on ice slides in winter, made sledges from spare pieces of wood, and collected sets of 'Cigarette cards' from packets showing famous cricketers of the time, Bradman, Verity, Washbrook, Compton, and of course Len Hutton 364 not out at the Oval in 1938. Like many other kids I also started a stamp collection.

On Holme Slack Lane there was a row of shops where you could purchase most things. Tea was 8d. (less than 4p) a quarter pound and you could buy five pounds of potatoes for 6d., (2½p). The shops included a haberdashery selling ribbons and buttons, braid, and materials; it's not a word much used these days, but it had added interest because it was owned by a former Preston footballer, Bobby Crawford and his wife. There was Bamber's Newsagents, sweets and tobacco, where the kindly owner used to hold out his hand to collect your money as a child, then as you gave it him he would close his hand round your wrist and pretend to pull you over the counter. But we soon learned to give him the money quickly then withdraw our hand with a giggle before he could grasp it. There was Shaw's chip shop with delicious fish and chips cooked in pure lard, none of the funny tasting smelly fats of these days for her! She was a large cheerful woman who would invite you to take salt and vinegar by asking 'Do you want any thingon?' I wondered for a long time what 'Thingon' was and whether you had to pay extra for it!

But it was the Co-op on the corner of Primrose Grove that I liked best. First came the Co-op butcher, then the main grocery shop. The counters were ranged down the right hand side and the end as you entered, and from various points there would be those wonderful aerial transport cables, all converging on a little cash kiosk high up in the corner of the shop to our left. The assistant would take your money for the groceries, write out a 'dividend' cheque, a pink strip of paper, worth 7½-10p in the £1, and put them into a little wooden container. He would then attach it with a single turn to a receiver on the cable, pull a handle and send it whizzing gloriously along the cable by a powerful spring action to the lady in the kiosk. She would receive it, check it and send it whizzing back with your change. There was even one that went through a hole in the wall to the butchers. It used to fascinate me and I used to wish I was small enough to be Tom Thumb to have a ride in it. There was a saying that the only way to get excitement in Preston was to go to the Co-op and watch the bacon slicer work, but I'd have settled for that cable system any day!

Horses and carts were still quite common on the streets of town and particularly in the outlying areas. Coal would be delivered by that means with a fully laden cart being pulled by an enormous Shire horse; and there would be great competition to be the first to gather up the 'coddy muck' on shovels for our roses, since it made marvellous compost. In town many of the hills were paved with stone 'sets' to give the horses a foothold in bad weather. Our milk was delivered by horse and cart. Farmer Metcalfe, whose farm was on Holme Slack Lane opposite Lily Grove, would come round with one of his friendly, laughing, ruddy-cheeked daughters, Nellie, Maggie or Mary, and they would ladle out rich creamy delicious milk from a huge churn into the jug which we took out to them. If we went round to the farm to collect it, it would be warm too.

There were rag and bone men who would push hand carts and shout 'Rag bone', and we could double our pocket money by getting a penny from the man in return for an armful of old clothes, which he would sell to the factories for oil rags. Once, I got over-zealous and gave him a pile that were actually waiting for the wash tub, and my mother had to rush after him and claim them back!

Another welcome visitor pushing a hand cart was the ever smiling Ice Cream Man. He wore a flat cap and seemed tiny behind that great cart, and we wondered how he could possibly push it up hill and down dale, for his depot was the other side of town. But it contained the most delicious ice cream a kid could ever hope to taste, and a cornet from him was a treat indeed. We could hear his call of 'Ice cream!' as he came up the lane, and even if we were cheeky and asked him 'What do you do when your mother hits you?', he would smile and shout 'Ice cream!'

Life insurance in those days meant the arrival at the front door once a week of the man from 'The Preston Shelley' to collect one penny for each member of the household. I well remember the time when my parents, seeing that the older twins had survived through wartime to reach working age, decided to cash the accrued sum, and the total of £25 was enough to buy them each a new bike from Chris Moss's in Fylde Road. How proud they were! We seldom saw them at weekends after that as they cycled to Chipping, Glasson Dock, Lytham and to every point of the compass. Norman wouldn't even go to the local shop 200 yards away except on his bike, and he was the same when he acquired a motor bike later!

We were in fact quite a motoring family. My father had an old Rudge motor bike, quite a powerful one with a side car, and he would manage to get all six of us on or in it by putting my elder sister on the pillion seat behind him, my brother on his own little 'dicky seat' with its own wind-screen in the front of the side car, and we younger twins would sit behind on our mother's knee. We went everywhere that way and were quite cosy.

Then later, my father bought a succession of old wooden bodied noisy, draughty Jowett cars, which needed all his ingenuity to keep them on the road. They were always breaking down or getting punctures on the unmetalled roads of those days, where sharp stones or thorny branches were a constant hazard. I remember quite clearly sitting on a raincoat on the side of a road, snuggling up to my mother with Marjorie and Doreen, all covered by a huge travelling rug as we watched my father being helped by my brother, who could have only been about twelve, as they jacked up the car and changed a wheel. I remember hearing Norman being complimented by my father for the help he gave, and my mother told us we all had to clap him. Our parents were such kind people. It's odd how rich little memories like that stay in the mind long afterwards.

Sometimes we would drive up to Tootle Height just beyond Longridge, a low hill where a brass band would play at the top on lazy sunny weekend days to entertain the strollers. We might then drive on round the shoulder of Longridge Fell to a small iron wicket gate which gave access to a field with lovely views to the west as far as Blackpool. I must have been about five years old then, and my favourite sweets were aniseed balls. Each of them was about ⅜ inch diameter, and you could buy a large cone-shaped paper bag full for ½d. So I could hardly believe my luck when, leading the way through this wicket gate I saw the grass sprinkled everywhere with aniseed balls! I was just popping one into my mouth when my mother, following up, saw the sheep in the field, realised what I was about to eat and stopped me just in time!

There was another hilarious occasion when we were all packed, ready to go on holiday to the East Coast, and our journey would take us over the dreaded 'Cat and Fiddle' pass over the Pennines from Macclesfield.

*Suddenly there was a 'whoosh' as the cork flew off, and there we were, with porridge all over the windscreen!*

Just as we were about to set off, a delivery boy on a big solid bike wasn't looking where he was going and crashed into the car radiator, which on such cars was open at the front, and was filled with water through a filler cap on the top outside. The cap was damaged and the radiator sprung a leak. So my father, ever resourceful poured in some oatmeal, knowing that when the water got hot it would swell and plug the leak; Holt's 'Radweld' wasn't around in those days. To replace the filler cap he used a large cork from a thermos flask. All went well until we started the long climb over the pass. As we climbed up and up the car got hotter and hotter, the pressure rose higher and higher and suddenly there was a 'Whoosh' as the cork flew off and there we were, with porridge all over the windscreen!

We used to like to drive to Fleetwood and time our arrival to the return of the very big fishing fleet, for there would be twenty or more trawlers in line astern, as Fleetwood was still a thriving fishing port. We would see the Isle of Man boats 'Mona's Isle' or 'Lady of Man' come in or go out, a very impressive sight to a small boy. There was a lighthouse in the middle of the street and I longed to see it lit but I never did, though I believe a single beam would be shone straight down the river channel when required to guide the ships as they approached.

Now another toy that my generous brother had passed on to me was a fine model sailing yacht which proudly carried the sign 'Clyde built'. It was indeed a beautiful model in fine wood with a sleek streamlined shape. So the huge boating pool at Fleetwood was ideal for sailing it, and it would go like the wind, invariably outpacing other yachts of its size. International model boat competitions were held there, but mine was a little too small and I was too young to enter - but I'd have bet anybody my Saturday penny that it would have won if I had!

At other times we would drive to Lytham for a walk along that fine promenade past the white windmill and by those lovely wide open greens. Sometimes we would go on to St. Annes and park by the pier and either play by that little kidney-shaped boating pool with our toy motor boats powered by a twisted elastic, or play on the sands. We might stroll round St Annes Square, where the beautiful and elegant shops rivalled anything in the more famous Lord Street at Southport. I always felt a sense of occasion when I went there; and used to look with wonder at that great statue group of Neptune holding his trident proudly aloft while driving a chariot with fine horses, that stood high on top of the Majestic Hotel. What a loss it was when the Majestic was demolished in 1975! Churchill had stayed there, and asked for soup to be brought to him at four in the morning when he worked late. Arnold Palmer and Jack Nicklaus were residents while playing the British Open at Lytham. Film stars Danny Kaye, the Marx Brothers, Kim Novak and Margaret Lockwood were its guests; and before he became famous as 'Geraldo', a young bandleader called Gerald W Bright had led his Majestic Celebrity Orchestra there. It was elegant, it was genteel, splendid, gracious, and a symbol of luxurious living which seems to have gone forever.

The hood of the car could be lowered and this was of course a boon at 'Blackpool lights' time. We would drive to South Shore then be routed with other cars all along the promenade past North Shore to Bispham, marvelling and gaping at the wonderful Illuminations between us and the sea. Brightly lit trams festooned with coloured lights would pass; there would be giant zig-zags of lights all the way up the tower, starting at the bottom and coming on in turn all the way up to reach a triumphant peak as the very top mast was illuminated. We would drive under colourful arches of lights across the road at intervals. There were tableaux of nursery rhymes with moving parts, and it became several miles of pure delight on a balmy night in late autumn. On the way back we would stop for fish and chips in Kirkham, then when we arrived home we would have to be carried into our beds fast asleep. It was a great joy to have such places within easy reach of home. In fact that is one of the great things about Preston – it is such a good centre for motoring. Within quite a short time we could be taking the sea air to the west, be up on the wild moors of the Trough of Bowland to the north east, strolling round the fine old abbey of Whalley or Clitheroe castle, or going beyond into Pendle Witch country. We could be climbing Darwen Monument to the south east; or driving into the market garden plains and across to Southport in the south west; and all offering quite different scenery.

We would go blackberrying around the lanes of Bleasedale and Chipping. My mother knew all the best places to look for them, and we would collect the lovely juicy berries, each of us armed with a jam jar with a carrying handle made of string. We couldn't resist eating some of course, but we'd still return home with several pounds of them for my mother to make fresh blackberry and apple jam.

When we went to Southport we would window shop in Lord Street then perhaps drive the car on the sands, and my father used to tell the story, probably quite unfairly, of the time he was teaching my mother to drive there, and in all that vast expanse of wide open sands she hit the only breakwater post still standing!

But equally, he was never allowed to forget the time we drove out to Hurst Green, beyond Longridge one chilly November morning, and he headed straight for a small cafe to order tea for us all. Meanwhile, the worthies of the village were gathering round the war memorial for the Remembrance day service. But he didn't notice that, and so he emerged suddenly from the tearoom, caught sight of us standing there and shouted 'Tea up!' - right in the middle of the two minutes silence!

Glasson Dock was a favourite with us, there were so many things to delight small children - capstans to climb on, lock gates to walk over, rusty old ships to look at, and all the cobbles, cables and clutter of a still busy port. If we camped at Conder Green nearby, the Stork Inn sold the most delicious real lemonade; there was an old wooden shipwreck along the shore to clamber over, and the turf was so perfect that men used to cut it for bowling greens and golf courses. We would watch the anglers fishing for fluke in the Lune Estuary and one of them didn't look behind him before casting and his hook caught in my sister Doreen's finger and made her cry.

Heysham was a popular place to visit because we could buy nettle beer from a cottage in the village. On Heysham head there was an amusement arcade, with a lovely old Victorian Disc music player, with a huge vertical circular steel plate with holes in it, which I think used to pluck reeds as it revolved, and it made a delightful hurdy gurdy sound. We would visit the ancient stone coffins on the headland, then think nothing of driving all the way back home to Preston on a chilly autumn evening with the car hood down. With petrol at only 1s. 7d. a gallon (about 8p) it wasn't a particularly expensive item. My father generally bought either Shell petrol or ROP which meant Russian Oil Products, because he thought the Jowett ran well on them.

I've previously mentioned the Yates's of Daisy Lane Holme Slack - Ron, Jack, and Peter and their parents. Ron and Jack were contemporaries of Tom Finney in the army, and my illustration shows them all in Egypt in 1944. It was Ron who reminded me that my father's Jowett was one of only two cars on the Holme Slack estate at that time, so it attracted a bit of attention. It didn't have a door lock, so one April Fools day the local lads pushed and steered it down to the bottom of Rose Lane Hill for him to find it there. To start the engine to drive it back he would then have had to switch on the ignition, and turn the starting handle at the front until the engine fired; taking care to have all the fingers and the thumb on the same side of the handle, for to leave a thumb on the other side was to invite a nasty sprain if the engine 'kicked back'.

Public transport from home to town when I was a small boy was both frequent and cheap. Buses would leave Holme Slack Lane about every seven and a half minutes during the rush hour and at no more than 15 minute intervals at other times. It would cost little more than a penny, less than half the present 1p piece, for the mile and a half journey. I remember that amount particularly because I was in town once and needed to answer a call of Nature so I had to make the ago-

*Tom Finney (centre) with Ron and Jack Yates in Egypt, 1944.*

nising decision to either spend the only penny I possessed, or take the bus home and hope for the best! I seem to recall that I chose the bus and that all was well in the event!

The route from Holme Slack to town would take the bus into Primrose Road, then across the Blackpool Road, past the Paragon Garage on the right, and the shop of Aloysius Hubbersty on the left, into St. Gregory's Road and along it. Then it would turn left into Skeffington Road, then right, into Harewood Road, and head west along St. George's Road. Crossing Deepdale Road it would then pass my granny's house on the right at the junction with St. Paul's Road: all the roads round there were named after saints – when someone said that that part of Preston was a 'saintly' place, they weren't kidding! The bus would turn left by St. Jude's Church and along St. Paul's Road past the Rialto cinema on the left, near the railway bridge, and join Meadow Street. There it would turn right past St. Ignatius Church, with its lovely white statue group which I much admired. The bus would then pass along North Road to Ormskirk Road where it turned right to join Lancaster Road near a big Co-op on the corner. It would then head south along Lancaster road towards Church Street and would park on one side or another of the Harris Library building, where many buses had their terminus, with covered bus shelters that nearly always held long queues.

Corporation buses served all parts of the town. Some buses had flat

*A bus waiting between the Harris Library and the Town Hall. Ashton buses had flat roofs.*
Photo by Harry Cottam

roofs and well-type walkways upstairs to reduce the height, to allow them to pass under the low railway bridge in Fylde Road. It was rumoured that one driver forgot and took a normal height bus down there, and got stuck, and that it was a twelve year old boy who solved the problem by suggesting they let down the tyres!

Outlying areas like Ingol and Woodplumpton would be served by 'Viking' buses. There were 'Scout' buses which served the Fylde, green Fishwick buses for the Leyland area, and Standerwick and Bamber Bridge Motor Services buses. Most of these operated from Starchhouse Square near Market Street, so there was plenty of competition to keep the prices low.

Ribble buses operated from Tithebarn Street, but access was difficult and they shared the street with the Fire Station, which of course had priority of use. Ribble buses travelling to Grimsargh, Longridge, Goosnargh, Ribchester, Kirkham, Blackpool, and places further afield into Yorkshire and Westmorland, would pick up and set down en-route through the Preston suburbs; thus giving the town very good public transport facilities indeed.

There would be Corporation bus stands outside many of the bigger factories, with direct routes to all parts to get workers to and from home as quickly as possible. But the cacophony of sound was incredible as workers who knew each other, and had probably chatted to each other

34

*Several bus companies operated from Starchhouse Square.*
Photo by Harry Cottam

all day, still found things to say while heading homeward! With only seated passengers allowed upstairs, as many as ten would be allowed to stand downstairs on those busy buses. Yet one would still see the old world courtesies as a man gave up his seat to a lady. If public transport was cheap and plentiful it was almost certainly because running and staffing costs were much lower than today, and there was an assured public support with fewer cars in competition. Those 'Special buses' were withdrawn in 1948 to a great outcry from people who didn't own cars, who would have to walk some distance from stops on the 'regular' bus routes.

Of course there were the trains too. The engines were big steam driven monsters. Most had names, some of them quite famous like The Royal Scot; and all had numbers which some train spotting kids would collect avidly. But I must confess I rather took them for granted. It is only since they have been replaced by diesels, which don't seem to have the same personality, probably because you don't see the moving parts – giant driving wheels, sliding connecting rods, and hissing steam any more, that I have missed them. The Preston LMS, London Midland and Scottish railway station was very much a main line station and a constant hive of activity; but you could also take local trains to all parts including Southport which lost its line some time later. It was an exciting place for a small boy and I hope it is still.

Once a year in those days before the Second World War there would be a 'Mayor's Fête' on Moor Park where each child would be given a present as he entered, a balloon usually. There were stalls, displays, competitions, brass bands, roundabouts, sideshows, bunting everywhere, a vast park filled to overflowing with thousands of people having fun. Also there were Co-op Field Days where each child got a lemonade or a currant bun, but which were much the same as the fêtes otherwise, and equally good fun on those long childhood summers when there seemed to be many more than 24 hours in a day, and all of them sunny.

Another memorable event which was held, this time on Avenham Park in 1935, was King George V's Jubilee after twenty five years on the throne. There was a most marvellous firework display, and I have a clear memory of looking back, as we walked up the sloping path towards Winckley Square, and seeing a whole sea of people as far as the darkness would allow.

Two years later at the coronation of King George VI there was a curious example of telepathy between twins when I arrived home from school just before Marjorie, proudly carrying the Coronation mug all we children had been given. I immediately sensed that she was in some sort of trouble, and that it involved her coronation mug. So I set off back towards school and sure enough, she had had an argument with another girl, and her mug had been knocked out of her hand and broken. I'm told I went at the other girl like Sir Galahad on his charger so fiercely that I made her cry. So my brother Norman gave Marjorie his mug, deciding I'd been a knight in shining armour quite enough for one day and I needn't give her mine! The older twins too were often clearly aware that something of moment was happening to their twin, even when separated by many miles.

The medical services in Preston during my boyhood seemed to work quite well. Doctor's waiting rooms were not unpleasant places, and I recall being mightily impressed when Dr Lytton's had that week's issue of 'The Beano' among the reading matter. But there were also some rather unfunny copies of 'Punch' magazine with overlong captions to the picture jokes - a carry-over of Victorian whimsical humour perhaps, with elaborate cartoons by Bernard Partridge.

If we needed the school dentist, we no longer needed to go to him as we had done in his surgery above Miller Arcade. He began to come to us at school, in a small specially equipped caravan which would be parked in the school yard. Depending on the work to be done we would have either 'gas', a total anaesthetic, or cocaine, a local one, which probably wouldn't be allowed now, though hopefully it was less harmful than the present drug. If we had a bigger dental problem, there was a facility off the waiting room of Preston Royal Infirmary where dental surgery would be done.

There were of course some delays in being seen to at PRI, they were usually very busy. But there were plenty of copies of *The Hotspur*, or *Adventure*, *Film Fun*, the *Dandy* or *The Wizard* comics available and there was always a pleasant cheerful atmosphere. Even today, the evocative hospital smell of disinfectant reminds me of that long corridor opposite the entrance, down which, as a small boy, I used to imagine the lame and infirm went and the healthily restored came out! My three day stay at the age of six to have my tonsils out remains in my memory only as a happy event, because I was allowed to keep the Dinky toy car they gave me to play with! Marjorie later had a most successful career there as a State Registered Staff Nurse and has fond memories of the hard but rewarding work of PRI.

CHAPTER FOUR

# Preston at War

A T THE AGE of sixteen in 1938 my brother Norman had been taken on as a trainee wireless operator by Walter Bibby, a friend of my father's, who was the Radio Officer on an oil tanker. On one of its journeys it went to Hamburg in Germany, and Norman came back with great foreboding, having seen hundreds of German troops massing in the port, a lot of naval activity and many Luftwaffe aircraft in evidence. He felt convinced, in spite of Prime Minister Chamberlain's 'Peace in our time' assurance, that the Germans were preparing to start something. So we had our own particular warning of what was to follow only one year later in 1939.

However, apart of course from those tragic families who lost loved ones; or whose family life was seriously disrupted by forced separation, which would affect childhood happiness too, I don't feel in retrospect that the Second World War affected Prestonians all that much. It was something we quickly learned to put up with. We were all issued early on with identity cards and gas masks, with special ones for the very young. The masks smelt very strongly of rubber, but we could breath quite well. We often had to practise putting them on and had to carry them around in their cube shaped, buff coloured cardboard box, with a string shoulder strap, wherever we went, even to sleep with them beside our beds at night.

Manchester and Liverpool had a much worse time; but I think we in Preston just got on with it. In spite of food and clothes rationing we didn't let it bother us too much. As a young child, I found it quite exciting and different, like an adventure story come to life. I could hardly be expected at that age to be conscious of the horror of it all.

I was 11 when it started on 3rd September 1939 and the family were again camping at Conder Green near Glasson Dock. We all crowded

38

into a railway level-crossing keeper's cottage to hear Neville Chamberlain announce on the radio that 'Since no undertaking had been received from Herr Hitler that he would withdraw his troops from Poland', which he had invaded that week, 'We were consequently now at war'.

Because we had a garden we were given an Anderson Shelter. If you hadn't a garden you got a thing called a Morrison Shelter for use inside the house. This was simply a strongly reinforced table with wire side netting between the legs. The flat top was apparently very good for table tennis except for the bolt heads round the edges! The Anderson shelter was a set of curved corrugated steel sheets which we had to assemble and bolt together to form an arch six feet long by four and a half feet wide by six feet high. There were straight sheets for the ends but it left a small open entrance for which my father constructed a strong reinforced steel door, which we could close, to be quite warm inside. We were instructed to dig a big hole about three feet or more deep into which the assembled shelter would be sunk. Then we had to pile sods and earth to a depth of about fifteen inches over the top of the shelter to provide further protection and also to help it blend more into the garden.

It wasn't long before the sirens went off for the first time, that awful up and down wailing sound like all the banshees in Hell; and of course we didn't know whether we were to be the target or not. Preston docks; the English Electric Company, rapidly converting to production of bomber aircraft from electric trams; the big mills, preparing to clothe the Forces and provide linen and bedding; all seemed very likely to attract the German bombs.

Generally, however, it was Liverpool or Manchester they were after. But our old dog Bess didn't wait to find out. As soon as the siren went off she'd be first in and last out of our shelter! Whether it was canine cowardice or just that she knew where the warmest spot was, we never knew, but her quick ear for the strange pulsating sound of those German bomber engines, a sound quite unlike our own, often gave us a minute or two extra warning.

There was room for all six of us quite happily in there, and my father was extraordinarily resourceful in building bunks down the side so that his children could go back to sleep. He put a paraffin stove in too, ventilated it, and even fixed up quite a good light, powered from a car battery; though we had to make sure nothing of that showed outside in the blackout, or the Air Raid Warden would have been down on us like a ton of bricks! So we would spend hours in there with not too much discomfort.

My mother always kept a basket of food ready to take in, saved from our 'rations', and we would come out only when the continuous steady

*We carried our gas masks in a cardboard box.*
Photo courtesy Trustees of Imperial War Museum

siren note of the 'All clear' sounded. I remember once, my twin and I were alone in the house when the siren went. As I hurried to get her into the shelter I heard the shrill whistle of a falling bomb and I waited for an explosion which never came. It turned out later that it was in fact an incendiary bomb which landed very conveniently on a rubbish tip between Holme Slack and Watling Street Road, just a few hundred yards away.

The day after, while searching for old pram wheels to make my trolley, I picked up what appeared to be an aluminium cylinder about fourteen inches long and two inches diameter. I took it home and asked my dad if there was any use for it on my trolley, perhaps as a roller or something. He went pale, grabbed it from me, stuck it in a bucket of sand, piled more on top of it, kept us all clear and called the Air Raid Warden and the police. It was the unexploded incendiary bomb. Being full, I believe, of phosphorus it could have burned me horribly. I protested that I didn't know what one looked like, it had lost the fins which would have made it look like a bomb, and I didn't know it had fallen there. But it didn't save me from a ticking off by all concerned that still rings in my ears!

We used to sing songs and tell each other tall and unlikely stories in that shelter. We would play 'I spy with my little eye' - though that didn't last long because there wasn't much in there; and my father would recount his adventures when he was a boy with his dog, Bruce. I think, looking back, that the shared risk brought us more together as a family, so the Enemy had his uses after all. I liked the story of the old woman in London when woken for the umpteenth time to be taken to the air raid shelter exclaimed, 'Ooh that Hitler - he is a fidget!'

On the very few occasions that German aircraft flew over the Preston area it was usually to approach Liverpool or Manchester from a different direction. Sometimes they would come in from the Irish Sea, having used the bright lights of the neutral Southern Ireland as initial aiming

CARELESS TALK
COSTS LIVES

*The wartime propaganda was quite convincing and often amusing.*
Photo courtesy Trustees of Imperial War Museum

points, before turning to attack Britain; or perhaps to avoid some of the barrage balloons, searchlights and anti-aircraft guns around our cities. We had several of all three forms of defence at Preston at first for a time, but I don't think they stayed long, perhaps they were needed more elsewhere. In any case the barrage balloons were only effective in preventing very low level bombing. They couldn't themselves be deployed to very great heights because the weight of their cables tended to drag them down, and the Germans just bombed from higher up.

Similarly the 'ack-ack' anti - aircraft guns were notoriously ineffective in spite of some determined effort by the gunners. But it made us feel better to see the searchlights sweeping the sky and to hear the distant sound of gunfire in our defence. If a bomber came our way it was probably because it was trying to escape our fighter cover; and it was one such, jettisoning its bombs to fly faster and get away, that demolished a house at Lostock Hall, causing one death and several casualties. There was a picture of it in the *Lancashire Evening Post* that made us think, 'There but for the grace of God go we'.

The propaganda that was broadcast and published throughout the war was pretty convincing and at times even amusing. When begging the populace not to disclose details of the war effort to anyone we would have slogans like 'Be like Dad - Keep Mum!' (which meant keep quiet). Or one of a blond woman surrounded by uniformed admirers with the motto 'Keep Mum, she's not so dumb' referring to the presence in our midst of German spies or sympathisers of the Nazis, who were known as 'Fifth columnists'; and throughout the factories there were posters showing a hard working man called 'Percy Vere' who was supposed to be an example to us all.

The iron railings round parks and public buildings were cut off at their base and removed to be used for the war effort. So of course we

41

*Norman was called up for the R.A.F.*          *Mother joined the Auxiliary Fire Service.*

told the younger kids the railings were going to be used as spears, because of the arrow heads on top, for when the ammunition ran out! In fact the metal turned out to be unsuitable for melting down for armaments and their loss was in vain.

I believe our family was typical of most in Preston during those war years of rationing and shortage. We managed on it and might even have been fitter for not eating so much! My mother joined the Auxiliary Fire Service and became the receptionist at a station in Ribbleton Lane. It was her task to 'put the bell down' when there was a call, and bring the firemen slithering down the brass pole through a hole in the ceiling from their waiting room above, who would man the appliances and go to the hastily scribbled address she gave them. We were terribly proud of our Mum whenever she volunteered to serve tea and refreshments from a mobile canteen to firemen and air-raid workers on Bootle Docks at Liverpool during the Blitz. We would look from an upstairs window at home and see the orange glow in the sky as that city burned thirty miles away, and wonder if we would ever see her again.

Doreen, likewise was the secretary to a director of Horrockses Mill during the day, but became a part time leading firewoman at the Tithe-barn Street station in the evenings. Until his call up for the R.A.F. as a wireless operator, spending most of the war in the Sultanate of Oman and Muscat, my brother served as a motor-cycle messenger for the Fire Service. He used to roll up on an impressive motor-bike with 'Fire' notices front and back that lit up. He was very proud of himself on that!

My father served in the Observer Corps and also as an Air Raid Warden. Marjorie was a tower of strength around the house during this time. My own little contribution at the age of twelve to fifteen was to help, along with my friends, as a cycle-messenger boy for the Air-raid Wardens in the evenings. We would wait in the basement of the Municipal Buildings in Lancaster Road, but were never actually called upon, so our table tennis improved enormously, and we had some very good picnics of Cornish pasties and mugs of tea, or fish and chips from Jackson's shop in Cannon Street.

There were hundreds of American airmen stationed in Bamber Bridge, and on Saturday evenings in Preston, we would see their Military Policemen, big burly men, absolutely immaculate in smart uniforms walking around in twos, usually one coloured, one white, to deal with any American who outstayed his welcome in the town's pubs. The three-pronged jibe that the Yanks were over-paid, over-sexed, and over here, seemed hardly fair to the troops in our area. Generally, they showed nothing but consideration and politeness and my father was mightily impressed when one of them, asking directions, called him 'Sir'. (One notable exception is described by Stephen Sartin in his interesting book, *Historic Preston*, published by Carnegie Publishing).

Several happy 'GI brides' left the Bamber Bridge area to start new homes in America after the war. It must be admitted however that Nylons were a problem. The original sheer silk stockings that women had worn before the war had long since become scarce because they were not a vital import, and they were only gradually being replaced by the new synthetic fibre Nylon material. So by about 1944, when we menfolk couldn't get near the fire for my sisters either doing their face or their hair in front of the big mirror over the mantelpiece, the question of what to do about stockings was a constant one for them. There were some Nylons in the shops I believe, but very few. They used up precious clothing coupons and were expensive, even more so if bought on the 'black market'.

The American GIs, as they were called, seemed to have access to Nylons from America, and some of the less scrupulous ones might try to use them for barter. The great majority of girls who couldn't buy them, and weren't prepared to go along with that arrangement, would buy bottles of light brown dye instead, and paint their legs to look as if they were wearing the sheerest denier Nylons. So in our house in those days there would forever be the pungent smell of those dyes, and the girls would then draw a line, with brown crayon, as straight as they could up the back of their legs to simulate the seam; and I wondered if their going to all that trouble was, perhaps, an updated version of the term 'Drawing the line' at the alternatives!

Flying Fortress B17 bombers were stationed at Warton near Lytham during the war and would be dispersed, bristling with guns around the airfield. Some were close enough to the Lytham road for a young aeroplane enthusiast to cycle over specially to gaze through the fence at those impressive war machines.

*Badge worn by the ladies of Preston Station Free Buffet.*
Courtesy Dorothy Blacow Satterthwaite.

But perhaps my most lasting memory of Preston at war was the Railway Station when a troop train came in. Platforms five and six, at that time, were to the left and right at the bottom of the ramp down from the entrance. They held fond memories for many a soldier from all over Britain, and I suspect that whoever has changed the numbering of those platforms since, didn't know that he was treading on the thoughts of many thousands of people.

Those fond memories were of the marvellous efforts of the women's voluntary services in serving free food and drink to tired, hungry and thirsty soldiers, during the all too brief ten minutes or so that those crowded troop trains stopped, either on their way south on platform five, or heading north on platform six. It was known as Preston Station Free Buffet.

If there isn't a plaque on each of those famous landmarks then I suggest there jolly well should be. Those women knew just when a troop train was to be expected, information that I feel sure the Germans would like to have had. As the train came steaming in they would swing smoothly into action, and ensure that every single passenger had a hot drink, something nourishing to eat, and a welcoming smile. The troops didn't need to get out of the train, everything would be handed through open doors and windows, and an entire train carrying hundreds and hundreds of men would be dealt with in those few precious minutes. I cannot recall a more impressive or moving sight.

Perhaps an hour would pass, then the whole thing would be repeated. It was a marvel of organisation and earned the gratitude of thousands of troops in every theatre of war, as well as bringing great honour to the town. The venture was funded by whist drives, beetle drives, raffles, auctions and every other possible fund raising venture in every church hall in the town. The wonderful ladies who ran the buffet were each presented with a commemorative mug when it finally closed, it hardly seemed sufficient, but they would not have wished for more. The thanks of thousands of grateful servicemen were enough.

To make food more readily available to hungry war-workers, 'British Restaurants' were set up in one or two parts of town. It can't have been easy, for rationing was quite severe. Yet the food was generally very good with commendable variety. A friend of mine, Fred Lang, tells the story that it certainly went down well with three kids he saw, gathered round one twopenny plate of soup, happily dipping pieces of bread into it and eating with great relish and enjoyment!

During the War the Preston Public Hall was pressed into service by the War Department. The Army Pay Corp. had the ground floor, and the balcony was used by clerks for recording and administering the lists of those killed in action, missing, taken prisoner, or admitted to hospital. They also took custody of the belongings of such casualties, among soldiers of some 18 regiments of north British origin. There was no heating on the balcony and the women clerks had to be issued with rugs in winter to keep out the cold. My second cousin Dorothy Blacow, of whom I have written, was an executive officer in that post and was later awarded the Queen's Coronation Medal for her services.

First Aid Posts were set up in and around the town which were manned by trained volunteers on a rota basis. In many cases they were those same ladies who on other days were helping in the Station Free Buffet. There was a marvellous spirit about the town in those wartime days, and everyone who could tried to 'do their bit'.

To allow for the possible loss of mains water for fire-fighting during an air raid, 'static water tanks' were built all over town. These were made of steel, were about fifteen feet long, six wide, and about six feet deep. It was soon found necessary to cover them to stop kids climbing up, falling in and not being able to get out. Saul Street Baths was also considered as a potential reserve supply in a crowded part of town. Now this could have been quite awkward because the place had a dual personality. On special occasions it would be boarded over by a prefabricated floor after being drained, thus losing its availability as a massive water tank. Then if a dance was to be held there, or a big band or orchestral show was arranged, it acquired its 'posh' name of The Queen's Hall.

It was there that I went to my first orchestral concert at Fred Lang's insistence. He was a school chum of mine. It was an ENSA concert, a wartime organisation that brought entertainment to the Forces and to people in the war industries. The orchestra was the Hallé from Manchester, under its conductor John Barbirolli. They played good rousing music like Wagner's Tannhauser, we didn't think of it then as German national music, and the soloist Eileen Joyce played the Tchaikovsky Piano Concerto. They also played Beethoven - loudly! The conductor's hair was all over his face at one point, and he delayed the start of one piece to turn round and glower at some late comers because he liked to educate his audience into proper concert-going manners! I thought it was great fun and couldn't wait for the next one which turned out to be vastly different.

It was a visit by the Liverpool Philharmonic Orchestra. Its conductor was a tall elegant man, immaculate in his attire, very upright and dignified. He was Dr Malcolm Sargent. His orchestra played the quieter music of Mozart, Elgar, and Delius and opened still more doors of enjoyment for me. The two orchestras came quite often after that, alternating, each with its own different repertoire of music. Some years later both conductors received deserved knighthoods and the 'Liverpool Phil.' became The Royal Liverpool Philharmonic.

But of course, with the best will in the world the hall was still a bath with tiled walls, and the acoustics were not of the best. So it was a great relief when the ENSA concerts were transferred to the New Victoria Cinema in Fishergate opposite the Miller Arcade. There we could sit in plush and tiered comfort to hear great music. So comfortable were they in fact that I fell asleep during Delius's 'The walk to the Paradise Garden' and got my leg pulled for paying good money for something that I could have done for nothing at home in the big chair!

Even there however, there was the possibility that we might have to evacuate if an air raid occurred. It was too risky to have so many people together, and we would be directed to one of the many public air raid shelters which were dotted around the town and in the parks.

My memory is vague as to how or when the big Victoria Mill in Deepdale Mill Street burned down. I don't think it was due to enemy action, but I do remember that my brother went along with his water pistol to help to put it out!

It was always easy to tell when a woman was a weaver in the mills. She would be an excellent lip reader, and would in turn move her lips in an exaggerated way to help others to lip read, because in the overwhelming clatter of dozens of looms in each shed it was the only way to communicate. Similarly the workers in the Royal Ordnance Factory at Euxton near Chorley had a yellow pallor to their skin, due to the cordite from the shells they made, which impregnated their pores. If a man was seen squatting on his haunches waiting for a bus, he was probably a Wigan miner, used to working in very confined spaces, with low head room before large cutting machines gave a man room in a mine to stand or sit as he wished. So we used to play a game of trying to tell a person's occupation by just watching them.

At night, the whole town would black out. No light was allowed to shine past our 'blackout curtains'. Car headlights would be covered by a grill that allowed only a small slit of light to shine downwards just in front of the bonnet so road speeds had to be reduced. Traffic lights were a mere slit of coloured light; street lighting was minimal; neon signs were banned, and you really had to know your way round the place after dark.

Preston must have been almost invisible from the air, but we dreaded moonlit nights when the reflection off the Ribble might give approaching bombers a line to the Docks and the factories nearby. Yet bombing of those targets never actually happened and life went on fairly normally. But there was always that extra dimension of camaraderie that comes from 'all being in it together'.

CHAPTER FIVE

# Working in Wartime

T HAT feeling of pulling together to help win the war, was not of course spoken about, but it was there just the same. Never more so that in the enormous factory of The English Electric Company, which filled most of the length of Strand Road, and stretched all the way back up the hill to Wellfield Road where the machine shops were. I don't think my memory serves me wrongly when I say that thirteen thousand people worked there during the war.

I had gone there aged 15 straight from school, and was eager to join in the fun because they made aeroplanes. When the war started in 1939, the company had been making electric trams, and soon, by a miracle of organisation they had converted to making giant Hampden Bombers. I joined them as an office boy in 1943 at a wage of seventeen shillings and sixpence (87½p) a week, and immediately got a taste of the pace of things when, after filling in my entry forms I was shown to the office where I was to work, past a long production line of aircraft. Shortly afterwards I had to return to the front office whence I came, and was asked if I could find my way. 'Oh yes,' I said, 'I noticed the number on the tail fin of that bomber opposite the entrance', thinking how bright I was. But they just laughed and asked if I realised that in the half hour that had elapsed, that aircraft could well have moved a hundred yards down the line, for they were producing seventeen of the things a week, about seventy a month! Seventy! - of those great big things! I decided there and then that Germany didn't stand much of a chance and may as well give up!

Work there was a reserved occupation and there was also 'directed labour', so once you were sent there you couldn't 'join up' into the forces even if you wanted to. You were needed there and that was that. Women were sent there from Glasgow and other cities. But men returning disabled from the forces would be given an honoured place on the payroll, and would wear their round 'George VI' recognition of service badge to show their status.

At English Electric there was twenty-four hour production. So if you were on certain shifts you might go to work in the dark, work your shift under those strange ethereal blue pear drops of light, then perhaps go home in the dark, and see real daylight for the first time only on Saturday. Even then it might be only for a few short hours in winter because Saturday morning work until noon was the norm in those days. But 'Double British Summer Time' helped in summer of course. J.B. Priestley wrote a book called 'Daylight On Saturday' about just such a factory as that during the war.

The Strand Road Works was a busy, active, bustling, yet very well organised place. Everyone seemed to know just what he or she had to do. It didn't surprise me in the least that that astonishing rate of production was maintained even when they changed to making a totally different aircraft, the Halifax Bomber. The sound of 'windy drills' and pneumatic riveters was terrific as one person, the 'holder up' would put in the cold aluminium rivets, and hold them in place with a special tool, while the person on the other side riveted them over. Then you would see the quality control inspectors going round drawing chalk marks round the rivets they didn't think were properly closed, and they would have to be done again.

Nor shall I ever forget the enormous Rubber Press. Women grouped round a big steel table would place flat sheets of aluminium onto shaped moulds. The table would then slide into the machine and be pressed up into a thick block of rubber which would form the sheets to the shape of the mould. Meanwhile another group of women on the other side were loading a similar table, and the tables would slide alternately into the press. They had to work hard and fast and most importantly as a team, for a delay by any one of them would hold up all the others. It must have been exhausting yet boring work relieved only by the cheerful *Music While you Work* radio programme broadcast especially for such busy war workers.

Aeroplanes in those days, like cars, were much less complicated than now. The main fuselage would start to be assembled at the northern end of the huge assembly shed of East Works, and as it progressed on wheeled frames other parts, assembled on either side, would be added to it. Of course the wings could not be attached or they'd never have got it out of the door! It was said however, that the whole length of the fuselage could have been turned into Marsh Lane if only a little old lady, who lived in the house opposite the exit, had allowed her house to be demolished to make room. It was said that because she didn't, the aircraft built there had to have an extra 'transport joint', to allow them

49

to be taken out in smaller sections and attached together later.

We were well aware, as we saw one of those giant aircraft going out of the big doors, that it was going to contribute directly to the war effort. It made all our own little contributions seem more worthwhile and gave us a lot of incentive to get on with it. But if we had forgotten that, there were the two brothers Alexander, each foremen of manufacture and assembly shops who ran their departments with military precision and kept everything running smoothly, who would certainly have reminded us! The efficiency, morale and motivation of the people in that factory was impressive to say the least!

Samlesbury airfield was used for final assembly and flight testing of aircraft later in the company's history, so it may have been that the Halifaxes were dealt with the same way. But unkind remarks such as 'when one of them flew over Germany and opened its bomb doors half the night shift fell out still playing cards' were not quite believed!

People were on 'piece work' so the more they did the more they earned; and there was the lovely story of Bill and Joe who would listen to the ratefixer's suggested terms of so much money per piece. Then big Bill, a huge burly man, would get very angry and shout 'let me get at 'im!'. So Joe would hold him back and say to the ratefixer 'hang on a minute, I'll try to calm him down'. He would then have a word with Bill, and come 'back and tell the ratefixer that if he could see his way to adding a bob or two to the rate, he could perhaps persuade big Bill to accept it. If the new offer still wasn't enough the performance would be repeated until finally, with a great show of reluctance, Bill and Joe would accept the final offer; knowing full well as the ratefixer went on his way, that they'd have happily accepted half his original offer in the first place!

But there were moments of great sadness too as wives who worked there to keep the home and family going would be missing from work one day, and we would learn that their husbands had been killed in action, or were missing, far out in the Western Desert. There was one particularly poignant moment when a workmate whom we called 'Bill fra Freckleton', a man with a most cheery smile, was approached by an ashen faced Foreman. He was told that an American Liberator Bomber had crashed onto the village school and playground in Freckleton, in spite of the pilot's frantic efforts to avoid it, and that his only child was among the twenty seven dead. Staff and pupils of the school were later buried in a mass grave behind the church.

It was a dreadful reminder that death could strike with awful suddenness in wartime. The Americans donated a children's play park to the village by way of small recompense but it only partially relieved the sadness felt throughout the area.

During the meal break, even on the night shift, entertainers sponsored by ENSA would come to the big canteen and put on a show. We even got Reginald Dixon with a small portable organ playing his famous signature tune 'Oh I do like to be beside the seaside' and other popular tunes. It was good that they did that as part of their war effort, and a funny comedian would send us back to our work still laughing at his jokes.

There was quite a bit of fun in the factory anyway. I had been taken on as an apprentice Toolmaker just six days before 'D Day' in 1944, and one of my first tasks was to operate a bandsaw which, if necessary, could cut long pieces of metal. For such a cut the other end of the piece needed the support of a 'stand'. I was told these came in two sizes, short ones and long ones, and I was sent to Stores for the long stand. The storeman listened to my request then said 'Hang on a minute I'll just have to serve this other bloke'. Then when it was my turn again he remembered something he'd forgotten to do, and so on and this went on and on until it began to dawn on me that I was just possibly being 'wound up'!

But I didn't fall for being sent for a bucket of blue steam I'm glad to say; and a friend of mine neatly turned the tables on the fitters when he was told to get a glass hammer and some rubber nails. He came back after lunch with a small solid glass hammer that was apparently used for very gently beating thin copper to avoid damage to the surface, and on the way back he'd called at Billy's joke shop in North Road and got some rubber nails.

If a man was due to get married he'd come in to find his overalls fly buttons sewn up. If he wasn't careful would find himself hoisted aloft by a crane hook through the back strap of his overalls just when he was about to leave, while all his mates would hammer a farewell on their benches. At Drydens, where Fred Lang worked, he operated a giant 'pit lathe' so huge that it was partly sunk into a pit to bring its working area level with a standing operator, and the idea was put around that it was even big enough to turn gasometers!

Even today it is possible to have fun with Lancashire humour. Quite recently I talked to a person who wasn't familiar with Lancashire expressions. The subject was toxic waste, and in mock seriousness I told him I was a bit worried about that stuff 'Nowt' that a well known firm of bakers takes out of its bread. I said that if they were that keen to get rid of it, it must be quite nasty dangerous stuff. I told him I had heard they were hoping to use the field behind his house as a disposal site, to dig a big hole to tip 'Nowt' into it, and he went away looking quite worried!

Our job in the Toolroom was to make the jigs and fixtures that held parts to be assembled or machined. It was precision work and often meant working to a fraction of a thousandth of an inch, so it was very interesting. I had the pleasure of working with a fine old fitter called Fred Moss, who had been kept on after he would normally have retired, because of his great craftman's skill. He could see at a glance if two faces of a piece of metal were not at right angles and could make things by hand that a machine could not have improved on. His wise advice on many matters had a great influence on me as an impressionable 16 year old, as indeed did the thoughtful wisdom of my father at that age. It was Fred Moss who got me out of a spot of bother when I had misread a drawing and machined too much off a valuable block of metal. An angry foreman had asked me if I knew there was a war on, but Fred said 'Aye but he's learned summat there an' I doubt if e'll do it agen'. That oil, poured on troubled waters, perhaps saved me my job.

The Toolroom was run by a remarkable Superintendent called Bill Harpley, a small man who always wore a trilby hat and who ruled the shop with a rod of iron, and scared the life out of anyone who stepped out of line. But he was a fair and just man who knew every part of the task and made certain that the aircraft production was not held up for lack of our contribution.

We had some fascinating tea-break conversations too. Russia was our ally during the war and it was quite normal to see the communist paper 'The Daily Worker' being shown around. There was a Preston branch of the Young Communists League, and I was forever having to argue with them, because I could not accept their atheistic views on religion, and most other aspects of their policies. So if only to try to show them there were other viewpoints, I would try to put the case for Christianity, because that was a powerful influence in Preston then, with literally dozens of active churches and thousands of church goers.

So, life in the toolroom was really quite a rewarding experience, and I still like to use my hands to make things. Though I was quite sorry to leave at the end of my training I had my sights on other things, the first of which was to transfer to the Jig & Tool Drawing office to design and draw the sort of things I had previously made.

As the need for massive production of those huge bombers receded towards 1945 the company transferred to the manufacturing of domestic appliances like cookers. At least that's what I thought. But once, when I went across Strand Road to West Works, a place I seldom visited, I was suddenly amazed to turn a corner and find myself face to face with the biggest railway engine I'd ever seen! The company was producing them for Indian State Railways it seems, and they had to be big and rugged to pull huge trains across that vast continent. So it showed the tremendous diversity of product of which that huge company was capable.

It was also about this time, that with the war almost won, a little aircraft was being made under contract and in great secrecy in a garage in Corporation Street, opposite the Public Hall. We called it the 'Doodlebug' after the V1 'Flying bomb' that had threatened to lengthen the war. In fact it was later called the De Havilland Vampire aircraft, one of our first jets, and soon after starting as a draughts-

*I was thrilled at last to be allowed to play some part in the design of the aircraft, and so achieve my boyhood ambition.*

man I had the honour of drawing up some of its first manufacturing jigs.

In the drawing office at lunchtime we had a very active 'Push-penny' league, in which one man would compete against another in trying to strike a penny piece with the back of a comb or a short ruler, to make it hit a halfpenny piece - the 'ball' - and hopefully force it through a goal, made from a bent paper clip, at his opponent's end of a polished table surface. It's surprising how seriously we took it, and success or failure was treated as a major triumph or disaster in our lives. There was even a silver cup for the winner of the league! Bob True, Ron Whitby, Ron Jenkins, Tom Hill, Norman Cliff, Colin Pimbley - a neighbour from Holme Slack Lane - Ron Bartley, Jack Shaw, Tom Swithenbank, Harry Thompson, Don Gill; fine draughtsmen all, keen competitors in the league, and good friends under our Section Leaders Fred Green, and Les Beardsworth, and Dennis Bickerstaff our 'checker'.

I knew the war was really over when those delicious triangular shaped 'Toblerone' chocolates appeared in the shops again; they were made in Switzerland I think, and were symptomatic of the many nice things of life we had missed during five and a half long years of war. It made us very thankful that we had come through it, and that its horror would now recede - yet we were still having to design jigs for military aircraft because, as we rejoiced at the end of the war, what Churchill described as an 'Iron curtain' was even then descending on Europe.

I had an interesting time in the Drawing Office, and by 1948 I was doing a set of twenty three drawings for jigs, to perform the sixty two machining operations on an aircraft undercarriage component which was so complex in shape that we called it 'Epstein', after the sculptor of that name. The aircraft which used that undercarriage unit was the *English Electric A1* the world's first jet bomber, later to be called the *Canberra* because I believe it was hoped to build some in Australia. It was designed at Warton (near Lytham), manufactured at Preston, and finally assembled at Warton.

By this time I had transferred to the Design Stress Office at Warton where I had gazed with so much interest at those wartime *Flying Fortresses* years before. This time I was armed with my shiny new Higher National Certificate with endorsement in Theory of Structures from Preston Technical College. I was thrilled at last to be allowed to play some small part in the design of that aircraft and its later versions, and so achieve my boyhood ambition, to see its very first flight in May 1949, and watch Roland Beamont fling it around the sky like a fighter aircraft with great flying skill.

What a joyous sight it was to see something on which we had worked for so long lift off the ground for the first time and exceed all our expectations - and on Friday 13th too! I well recall the tremendous noise made by its twin Avon jets on take off, as we stood on the airfield. As the sound faded when it flew out over the Ribble estuary, it was replaced in the silence that followed, by a skylark which started up as if to say 'If you've quite finished - I was here first!'.

But it was because I felt I wanted to know more about other aspects of aircraft, that I left Preston two years later in 1951 for further study, thus bringing to an end my working life in Proud Preston.

## CHAPTER SIX

# Preston Scientific Society and Preston Camera Club

M Y BUDDING interest in photography and science in general from about 1943 had led to my being invited to join Preston Scientific Society, which met in Ellesmere Chambers above a bank in Church Street. A learned society it certainly was, but was never dry or dull, and the lectures and demonstrations by experts in their particular fields were always well presented and delivered. I took a special interest in the photographic section which was then run by a Mr. Ovenden, one of nature's gentlemen, who organised photographic outings and practical sessions on photo techniques.

In due course I became the section treasurer and that experience of committee work was valuable when I later also joined Preston Camera Club. It met in rooms above a shop in Cheapside and I became its Syllabus Secretary. I recall that one of my happier choices of speaker, a man called Swindlehurst from Nelson, astounded us with the sheer beauty of his photographs of the bleak Pennine Moors. Perhaps just a single tree on a rugged skyline with a glorious sunset behind it, or the image of a tousled sheep reflected in the waters of a moorland pool. He showed that there were pictures all around us if we just looked for them, and opened our eyes to what we were missing by just taking snapshots of people all the time. But we did hold proper portrait sessions occasionally, when an attractive young lady wearing a pretty dress would sit for us.

Another, but less happy occasion was the visit of one Lancelot Vining, a regular contributor to the popular magazine 'The Amateur Photographer'. His articles on 'My Way with the Miniature' were widely read, for the 35mm camera which was much less common then and considered very small. Because of his fame we hired a big room over the Co-op in Ormskirk Road and invited the Mayor to attend and introduce the speaker. Lancelot Vining turned up in an old tweed jacket and corduroy trousers, and was shocked and annoyed to see such a vast audience and the Mayor there too in pin-stripe suit. He explained through clenched teeth that he had thought he was just going to come and perch on the edge of a table and have a small chat to a few fellow enthusiasts and show a few slides! I should have told him of course, and I had to apologise. But once he was reconciled to the situation he was much more expansive and gave an excellent and amusing talk on the perils of life as a photo-journalist in Fleet Street. At the end he admitted that he had in fact been quite flattered to see such a turn out, and hoped that the amateur photographers of Preston would continue to flourish.

This in fact they did, for the club became known far and wide in the county for the pictures it produced in those early post war years. Again I was not alone in finding that my fellow members had also made a lot of their own photographic gadgets during wartime shortages, and had produced excellent results with them.

## CHAPTER SEVEN

# Preston Lads in the Lake District

DURING this time - the mid '40s - Fred Lang and I, together with a lad whom we always called 'Buckwheat' for no good reason, and another lad called Eric Ward, used to go Youth Hostelling in the Lake District. We climbed most of the great mountains, Scaefell Pike, Bowfell and the Crinkle Crags, Helvellyn, the Langdales and many others, often in quite hostile weather, and returned to one of the several hostels for the evening usually for a marvellous sing song around a log fire. Our favourites were Longthwaite Youth Hostel in Borrowdale, and Thorny Howe at Grasmere. But a particular farmhouse in Wastdale had a special place in our hearts. We had traversed the Sty Head Pass in atrocious weather and arrived wet to the skin at the Wastdale Head Hotel. There we were told that they couldn't make us cups of tea because they had no water - though we'd been almost swimming in the stuff all afternoon. So we tramped on to the farm and had the most delicious tea with a table piled high with home-made scones and cakes, toast and pancakes, and hot steaming tea, then went on to Wastdale Youth Hostel. What a lovely way to end a day that was!

We were in Ambleside once, sitting in Dodd's cafe, at the end of such a hostelling holiday and I was anxious to know if I had enough money left for both the bus home to Preston and a snack and maybe a postcard or two to show to my folks. So I spread my entire revenue on the table before me. Just then, the waitress came along to clear the table before taking our order, and I saw her eyes sparkle as she began to collect what she thought was a generous tip left by a previous customer. So with a wit born of sheer desperation I piped up and asked if we all had to pay for our meal before we had it! Fortunately she got the message and the day was saved.

There was, and still is, a magic about the Lake District which makes it quite unlike any other part of Britain. I think the slate and stone buildings help, and of course the people there are friendly and tolerant, but there's something about the light there, soft, luminescent, often with a gentle mist, that gives the place a fairy tale atmosphere. Yet those mountains can be very unforgiving to anyone who takes them for granted, or who ventures out ill equipped. The weather on the tops can change from bright sun to swirling cloud, icy wind and lashing rain within half an hour.

We were in Keswick the day the whole war ended – 'Victory in Japan, VJ Day', in August 1945. Of course we celebrated and that evening at the youth hostel at Patterdale on Ullswater we joined an impromptu dance with all the young lasses we could find in the village and had a whale of a time. Though we were properly kitted out, we were rather unwise when the four of us set out the following day to climb Helvellyn, to traverse the dangerous narrow sharp razor edge of Striding Edge and return back down Swirrel Edge, when we were probably seeing two of everything!

Later, when we'd learned a bit more sense, some of us joined the prestigious Preston Mountaineering Club and rock climbed on Dow Crags above the Coppermines Youth Hostel at Coniston. It usually fell to me to take photographs of the climbers preparing to climb, or in action on the rock face. This, of course, meant that I had to be up there alongside them, belayed to the rock and holding on with one hand while taking pictures with the other, and I had to remember not to ask them to step back a yard or two so that I could get them all in the picture!

In May 1948, five of us, all from Preston, Ron Jenkins, Fred Champion, Stewart Campbell, Bob True and I, camped by the shore of Esthwaite Water. It was the May Queen village festival, with a Maypole in Hawkshead, and at the dance in the evening the newly crowned May Queen was supposed to have had the first dance with the Chairman of the Rural District Council. But one of our party, who shall be nameless, was a personable lad, and he and the young lady had to be found and virtually prised apart from somewhere round the back of the hall, so that she could perform her civic duty!

The following evening some of us decided to sleep out all night on the summit of Coniston Old Man. Three of us, Ron, Fred and I climbed the mountain while Bob and Stewart stayed to guard the camp. We built two walls of stone on top as wind breaks, watched the sun go down over Ravenglass then bedded down for the night. I was just going off to sleep when Fred nudged me and asked 'Do you want to buy an elephant?' So of course I said 'No thanks, I'm trying to give them up, my Dad says they're a bad habit'; and I was just nodding off again when Ron observed that 'At that moment we were probably the highest people in the land!' 'No we're not' said Fred 'The King is – go to sleep!' We were a bunch of carefree idiots in those days.

We were finally wakened by baying foxhounds jumping across our stone walls. So we got up, watched the sun rise over Windermere, lit a fire with the wood we'd brought up with us, wished we'd brought more because our billy-can didn't boil so we drank cool soup, then went down to the village at 8am. There, a nice old gent asked 'Going hiking lads?', 'No', we said, 'We've been!'

## CHAPTER EIGHT

# Entertainment in Preston

P RESTON was well served with theatres and cinemas during the 'thirties and 'forties, and at one time or another we went to them all. The
Theatre Royal in Fishergate had been a theatre but had changed early
on to being a cinema. The Royal Hippodrome in Friargate, not far down
from the market place, remained the main venue for Grand Opera,
comic and light opera, and repertory theatre. Famous names such as the
great tenor Richard Tauber appeared with Charles Hawtrey in 'Old
Chelsea'. The well known actor Frederick Jaegar learned much of his art
in repertory there, in a different play each week for a whole season.

I have mentioned my school friend Fred Lang; he had a happy knack
of always doing worth while things and introduced me in turn to Scouting, to photography, to the Lake District and its fells, to orchestral music,
and to opera. I owe him a great deal for enriching my life in that way. He
insisted I go to a performance of 'La Boheme' given by the Carl Rosa
Opera Company, and I loved every moment of it. They returned later to
perform La Traviata, Madam Butterfly and other famous operas, so a
visit there became an occasion to be relished. The original Doyly Carte
Company would visit regularly with the Gilbert and Sullivan Savoy operas and we would go home humming the catchy tunes and looking
forward to the next visit.

Fred himself was no mean pianist, and when I visited him in his house
at 312 Brook Street he would play Beethoven's Moonlight Sonata with
great feeling, or put on records of 'The Barber of Seville' and other
Rossini overtures. It is amazing what enjoyable artistic experiences
were possible in private houses, halls and theatres around the town in
those days before television insisted its way into our lives.

There were also the Blackpool theatres of course and we would travel
there in anything on wheels if there was a famous artiste visiting.

Shortly after the war a group of us from Preston saw the famous tenor Beniamino Gigli at the Winter Gardens. He had been a great favourite with the British forces in Italy apparently, with his song 'Come back to Sorrento', and now here he was in person. His programme included about ten operatic arias, then because the audience wouldn't let him go he sang no less than thirteen encores!

The Kings Palace Theatre near Tithebarn Street was still very active as a Music Hall before television brought its demise. Names spring to mind, such as Anne Ziegler, Webster Booth, Wee Georgie Wood and G H Elliot (The Chocolate Coloured Coon), singing his famous song 'Lily of Laguna'. Sandy Powell, 'Can you 'ear me Muther?' and Frank Randle 'I'm happy when I'm hiking' were popular acts. Max Miller would try to shock us with his blue jokes; Hetty King, male impersonator, smoked a pipe as a sailor, and Old Mother Riley came on with her 'daughter' Kitty. Norman Evans would lean 'Over the garden wall' - 'Eeh that cat, it does smell, I could smell it in't custard this mornin'; Albert Whelan would saunter on whistling a tune that became all his own - the first man ever to use a signature tune - and Dante the Magician was a source of total wonder. Having raised a young lady horizontally off a couch, so that she hung motionless without visible support, by means of 'levitation'; or sawn a woman in half, and passed between the two halves, while she still moved her head and wiggled her toes, then having put her back together again, he would spread his arms and shout 'Sim Sala Bim!' triumphantly.

The Western Brothers were pure cynicism in evening dress; the young Frankie Vaughan made some of his earliest appearances, Jack Warner, and his sisters Elsie & Doris Waters - 'Gert and Daisy' and many more brought joy and laughter and the thrill of seeing these famous people 'in person'.

There were amateur theatre productions all over Preston too; musical comedies, plays, concerts, choral events, even Scout Gang Shows in the style of those produced in London by Ralph Reader, including what we called 'The Surfer's Song' - 'We're Riding Along on the Crest of a Wave'.

The marvellous Public Hall in Corporation Street put on annual performances of Handel's 'Messiah' with huge choruses of local singers, and famous soloists, with Preston Symphony Orchestra conducted by an enthusiastic lady musician. I have often wondered if our own wonderful Kathleen Ferrier, born in Higher Walton in 1912 ever sang there. It would have been no more than that splendid hall deserved, with its fine organ swelling out proudly in accompaniment of great singing. After the war the Liverpool Philharmonic and the Halle Orchestra often played there, so that a visit to that superb Hall always made a most memorable evening. When a famous Polish pianist came to the Public Hall to play Chopin, my mother, who in her quiet way did everything she

61

could to encourage her children's interests, presented me with a ticket which she'd gone specially to town to buy, because she knew I'd like to attend. When I saw the price, it was 7s. 6d., a very large amount then, and I realised she'd given up a large part of her housekeeping to pay for it.

Occasionally there would be a visit to Moor Park by Bertram Mills Circus, a spectacular and much anticipated event. We would watch the parade to the site with the elephants padding along, trunk to tail; clowns, horse riders and performers all giving us a preview of the excitement to come.

We would watch the 'Big Top' giant marquee go up, a marvel of co-ordinated effort, then perhaps see some of the artistes practising outside. There were always bright colours - gorgeous reds, startling yellows, rich royal blues, gold, and deep purple and iridescent lights - all adding gaiety to the scene.

The show was sheer magic for a young child. There would be the ringmaster in a bright red tail coat, white bow tie and top hat, who would introduce the acts in a booming voice. The band would play 'Entry of the Gladiators' and in would come the clowns, ridiculous in their big shoes, funny red noses, feathered hats and baggy trousers - which would usually get water poured down them at some stage - to peals of laughter from the kids. There were flying trapeze artistes in glittering costumes, turning over and over though the air, to be caught with split second timing by the outstretched arms of their companions. There would be magnificent circus horses trotting round the ring, with girls doing acrobatics on their backs. Then there would be the tumblers, building huge pyramids of people and one would jump on one end of a see-saw, to make someone at the other end fly somersaulting in the air to land at the very pinnacle of the triangle.

Fierce Bengal tigers would share a cage with proud maned African lions, with a fearless tamer who always had to look out for an attack if his back was turned. There were performing dogs which would jump through hoops, and dance on their hind legs. There were sea-lions that could play 'God save the King' on a row of trumpets; and best of all, if you were near the front you would be invited into the ring by one of the clowns, and do somersaults with them, or be allowed to throw a bag of flour at another clown, and you would get a balloon as a present when you went back to your seat.

It was all glitter, noisy 'alley oops', 'ta ras'!, applause from delighted children and their parents, crashing of cymbals, drum rolls at special moments of skill, and a pure escape to another exciting world. It was wonderful, it was marvellous and there was no other experience quite like it!

Furthermore if you went to the Tower Circus at Blackpool you could see the legendary 'Doodles' one of the all time greats among clowns, or the Carolli Brothers. There would be a spectacular finale when the whole ring would be lowered to let in water to form a circular pool with fountains. On the central dais would be beautiful girls performing a water ballet, and sometimes they would be painted from head to toe in gold.

If you had been to a matinee and emerged onto the Promenade, you might be fortunate enough to see another form of gymnastics - aerial gymnastics as one of the marvellously manoeuvrable biplanes of those days trailed smoke as it traced out an advertisement for 'Rinso' or 'Persil' in letters two hundred yards high in the still air. It was called 'Skywriting'.

There were at least eighteen cinemas in the town, five of them in Church Street and Fishergate. The New Victoria opposite the Miller Arcade in Church Street had a Wurlitzer Organ which used to rise up out of the depths to play, then descend again when the film started, and the man gave my twin a ride on the seat as it went down on one occasion. To the left, beyond the Parish Church and in Church Street on the same side was the newer Ritz Cinema. Opposite, and almost side by side were the Palladium and Empire cinemas. We would go to the latter for Saturday matinees and pay fourpence to sit in the circle and watch Flash Gordon defeating the mighty Ming Emperor on some distant planet. Or we would watch films of Laurel and Hardy, or Charlie Chaplin. At the top of Fishergate Hill, just beyond Theatre Street and before the train station, was the Theatre Royal already mentioned. Perhaps seeking to retain their reputation as a former theatre, they tended to show the more discerning films.

Further out of town were the star Cinema at the corner of Corporation Street, Fylde Street and Fylde Road - the first cinema to show 'talkies'. In New Hall Lane there was the Plaza; while nearby in Tunbridge Street next to Acregate Lane was the Queens. The Carlton was in Blackpool Road near Ribbleton Avenue, an easy walk over 'the forty steps' from Holme Slack, and our next nearest cinema was the Rialto in St. Paul's Road, a smaller building which seemed to shake a little as a train went by out of the tunnel on the Longridge line. Nurses from the nurses' home at the nearby infirmary would go there in their time off - which seemed as good a reason as any for us lads to go there too! The Guild in Geoffrey St., the Picturedrome in Brackenbury Place, the Empress in Eldon St., and the Princes at the corner of Tithebarn St. and Crooked Lane were all in full operation; as was the Savoy in Ashton Street, an unusual building with a castellated turret at the front corner. The Regal in March Lane, renamed the Lido, tried to keep afloat by showing interesting foreign films, but few if any of these out of town cinemas survived the onset of television in the home, yet they had usually shown their films to quite full houses, and changed their programmes twice a week. We would watch Tarzan films with Johnny Weissmuller, an Olympic medal winning swimmer, in the part, saying the same word 'Umgowa' for every command, whatever he wanted, and getting a different response from every animal he said it to, and swinging from tree to tree on conveniently placed creepers. There were Sabu the Elephant Boy, Shirley Temple of course, Charlie Chan, Gene Autrey the Singing Cowboy, Errol Flynn as Robin Hood getting the better of Basil Rathbone who was 'Sir Guy of Gisburn', and a host of other Hollywood stars. When I was a bit older I was in love with Ingrid Bergman - those eyes!, and Kathryn Grayson for her gorgeous husky voice, both at the same time, and would watch repeats of their films wherever they were shown in Preston.

But we didn't neglect British films such as 'The Wicked Lady' with Margaret Lockwood, and I

### WORSLEY'S BALLROOM
**Market Street, Preston.**
'Phone 4961

## Weekly Programme

MONDAY—Public Dancing 8 p.m.-11 p.m. to our band.
Admission 2/-

WEDNESDAY—Public Dancing 8 p.m.-11 p.m. to our band.
Admission 2/-

THURSDAY Afternoon—3 p.m.-5 p.m.
Dancing with Instruction. Admission 1/6.

THURSDAY Evening—KEEN DANCERS NIGHT.
Latest variations. Team matches, Competitions Etc.
A good practice night for dancers.
8 p.m.-11 p.m. Admission 2/-. (Dancing to sound equipment).

FRIDAY—Special Instruction Class and Dance Practice.
A good night for beginners. Waltz, quickstep, foxtrot and tango taught. 7-30 p.m.-10-30 p.m. Admission 1/-.

SATURDAY Afternoon—Special Instruction Class for beginners and Advanced Dancers. 3 p.m.-5 p.m.
Admission 1/-.

SATURDAY Night—Popular Dance Night to our band.
8 p.m.-11 p.m. Admission 2/-.
Private lessons from 10-0 a.m. to 7-0 p.m. by appointment.
Medalist classes also by appointment.

PRINCIPAL—Madam E. M. Worsley,
Fellow U.K.A.P.T.D.
Member M.A.T.D (Northern Area Chairman)
CECIL RAW, Fellow U.K.A.P.T.D. (Highly Commended)
Member M.A.T.D (Northern Area Secretary)
Member I.S.T.D. Inc (Comm.)
Member B.A.T.D.
MARGARET WORSLEY, MEMBER M.A.T.D.
and Qualified Staff.
Coaching for the Profession.
Adjudications — Demonstrations.

**DANCE AT WORSLEY'S**
PRESTON'S BEST BALLROOM.
To Preston's Best and Brightest Band.
**ALL CATERED FOR - ALL WELCOME.**

*Worsley's ballroom was particularly popular among teenagers.*
Courtesy Albert Evans

was always interested to see my namesake, Michael Wilding on the screen. Films like 'Brief Encounter' with Trevor Howard, 'In Which We Serve' with Noel Coward, and the Will Hay films were all classics and all from British studios. It is surprising too how well those old films have stood the test of time and are still shown on TV with great success.

Dances would be held in venues all over the town including the Annual Works Dance in the public hall. Worsley's ballroom in Market Street was particularly popular among teenagers. It was kept strictly respectable under the control and patronage of its Principal, Madam E. M. Worsley. It was a good place to meet nice girls, and you weren't necessarily expected to arrive with a steady girlfriend - you could 'play the field' as we called it, and if anyone was a bit shy, or something of a wallflower, the staff, whom we affectionately called 'ice breakers', would gently introduce couples to each other and encourage them to dance, so that we all enjoyed ourselves and got to know lots of people.

The usual dances then were the quickstep, the foxtrot, the waltz, the tango, the samba, the palais glide and the Old Time dances such as the veleta and the barn dance. There were even small halls such as the Park Ballroom near Winckley Square, where you could learn to dance privately with understanding girl hostesses who presumably wore reinforced toe caps! Of course the most popular orchestra to learn to dance to then was Victor Sylvester's Ballroom orchestra. It is only necessary for anyone of that generation to hear a few notes of his music, for them to take on a wistful look and think of those days of 'Slow, slow, quick quick slow!', and those fumbling steps as we tried to avoid tripping over our own feet or standing on our partner's.

Four former Preston Grammar school lads, Harold Walkden, Percy Kendrick, John Brooks and Herbert Alston formed a promotional group called 'The Four Aces' who ran a dance club. One evening they would organise a Gala night - 'no one admitted without a smile'; another, a Boogie Ball, for 'Boogie woogie' was very much the music of the time. Another winter evening there would be a 'Snow Ball', with Father Christmas and a snowball fight; and yet another there would be a Carnival Night, or a Lucky spot dance, with prizes. Each of the Four Aces would be Masters of Ceremony in turn and the venue would be the Queen's Hall, or St. Ignatius Hall behind the church.

Our Scout group also organised weekly dances in Broughton village hall and these too were always well attended. We would sprinkle French chalk on the floor to make dancing easier, and an item of opera or classical music would be played in the interval for a change of mood. When 'Square dancing' came over from America our Rover/Ranger group formed a demonstration team and went round the clubs showing them the steps, and we would wear the authentic check shirt and jeans - shades of dear old Miss Pritt! But at all these dances it was the tradition to end the evening with The Last Waltz when you were all nicely sleepy; you would always reserve this one for the girl you really liked, and would like to walk home with, so there would be a nice dreamy romantic slow waltz to end another pleasant evening of dancing.

If we stayed at home in the evening we could hear other famous bands on the radio, for it was the era of the Big Bands - Jack Hylton, Geraldo and his orchestra, Jack Payne, Ambrose, Roy Fox, Joe Loss with 'In the Mood'. Oscar Rabin, Carol Gibbons, Ted Heath and his band, Cyril Stapleton, The Squadronaires, Felix Mendelssohn and his Hawaiian Serenaders, Trois and his Mandoliers were all very popular. Billy Cotton's Band used to play 'Somebody Stole my Gal' as their signature tune. Henry Hall's Guest Night used to sign off with 'Here's to the Next Time and a Merry Meeting', and Mantovani came along later with his 'singing strings'.

A popular American band was, of course, Glen Miller with his 'Moonlight Serenade', 'Little Brown Jug' and other great numbers; it was a loss to us all when he took off in an aircraft in wartime and was never seen again, but his music has lived on to entertain us ever since. Before him there had been Tommy and Jimmy Dorsey, Count Basie, Duke Ellington, Benny Goodman and many more, all legends now, but day to day listening then. Bing Crosby's style of singing was called 'crooning', and much later Frank Sinatra appeared too, singing in films and on records.

There were radio programmes such as 'In Town Tonight', interviewing visiting celebrities and 'Band waggon' with Arthur Askey and 'Stinker' Murdoch – we never did find out why they called him that! Arthur would call us 'Playmates' and sing his silly Busy Bee song, and 'Monday Night at Eight O'clock' was a popular weekly programme. Albert Sandler and his Palm Court Orchestra would serenade us on a Sunday evening, with their signature tune 'Roses from the South'. Tommy Handley's ITMA – 'Its that man again' was always very funny – 'Can I do you now Sir?' asked Mrs Mop, and TTFN 'Ta ta for now' entered the English language. And of course the Goon Show was a dafter form of humour than we'd ever heard before, with Eccles, Bluebottle, Major Bloodknock and Neddie Seagoon. Reginald Foort would entertain us on the BBC Theatre Organ and he was followed by Sandy MacPherson and occasionally Reginald Dixon from the Blackpool Tower Ballroom. As much younger children we had listened to 'Toytown' with Larry the Lamb and Mr. Growser – 'It's disgrrraceful!' he would say, and even earlier we had listened to 'Teddy bears' picnic' or 'I'm Burlington Bertie' on headphones on my father's *Cats Whisker* wireless set.

I clearly recall listening to the first ever Christmas broadcast by a reigning monarch, King George V. His Silver Jubilee in 1935 was an occasion for great rejoicing. We heard the Abdication broadcast of his son Edward VIII, which My mother was very sad about because she thought he was very handsome and debonair, and kept a photograph of him on top of the piano in the sitting room. We listened with sympathy to the Coronation broadcast in 1937 of his brother George VI, for he had been thrust into the limelight with little preparation, and it was even more difficult for him because he had to control a stutter. The new King later visited Preston and we schoolkids were lined up all along Moor Park Avenue to see him drive past, and gave him a great reception.

'Gramophone records' as they were called were all 78 revs per minute, very scratchy, and broke if you dropped them. One side would give about four minutes play. The stylus was a steel needle or there were thorn needles which wore the record less but were not so loud, and didn't last very long. Most of the entertainers past and present made records; Gracie Fields was at the height of her fame, Paul Robeson with his deep rich bass voice singing 'Old Man River' and 'The Canoe Song' from Sanders of the River; Richard Tauber with his 'You are my heart's delight'; and a young Jussi Bjorling with that most melodious voice of his. Vera Lynn of course – 'The forces' sweetheart' reminded the lads of home. Flanagan and Allen sang 'Underneath the arches', 'Run rabbit run' and many more in that 'not quite in harmony' style of theirs.

We had several older 'white label' records too of the great Italian tenor Enrico Caruso, which my parents particularly liked, and of Madam Tetrazzini who sang Mozart rather well. Our family favourite record was 'The Desert Song' and it happened to be about the fifth from the top in a pile of records which someone accidentally sat on and it was the only one that broke! My brother suggested that was because we had played it so often it was thin enough to play the other side backwards!

All these records we listened to before the new long play thirty three and-a-third revs per minute 'full fidelity' discs came on the scene, and prompted the story of the exasperated wife who complained to her husband that if he didn't stop playing his new 'High fidelity, low frequency' record player, and pay her more attention, she would go in for low fidelity at high frequency! Those scratchy, noisy 78 rpm records didn't begin to compare with the long play and more modern compact discs, but we enjoyed listening to them, for it was all we had.

The proprietor of a domestic appliance shop called Bateman and Baxters in Friargate started a classical music evening club on his premises. He made a scroll-shaped backdrop to his record player and it had hidden coloured lights which could be slowly turned on in various combinations to suit the mood of the music, purple for Elgar's noble music, golden for Bach and so on. It was a very effective early audio visual show, very entertaining and much appreciated. So we didn't mind at all when he advertised his Bendix Washing Machines in the interval, because we were sure that wasn't only why he ran those musical soirees – he just liked others to share the pleasures of good music with him.

Apart from the fact that many of us were going to 'night school' at the Technical College three nights a week in winter, and doing homework for another two, there was still plenty to do in the bit of spare time we got in Preston.

It is surprising how one's sense of smell can stir memories. Whenever I smell the delicious aroma of freshly ground coffee my mind shoots back to Saturday mornings at the Kardomah Cafe on the north side of Fishergate. There was always that lovely tang of coffee in the air, and the place had retained a lot of its old style even after the war when we were in our late teens.

There were still the separate cubicles with polished wooden partitions, and red plush seats with gold edging, to give privacy for those who wished it. But it was to the balcony that we headed. Here we could meet friends of our own age and interests, members of the Rover/Ranger group, people we hiked and rock climbed with, or girls who came to the dances at Worsley's or Broughton.

*Whenever I smell the delicious aroma of freshly ground coffee my mind shoots back to Saturday mornings at the Kardomah Cafe on the north side of Fishergate.*

We would plan new outings to the hills, cycle rides, tennis matches, and visits to the cinema or the theatre; none of that shyness now, that was long gone, the conversation sparkled and we were all happy to see each other. We seemed to be into every activity available, so there was never a dull moment and life was very good in Preston then.

CHAPTER NINE

# Social Attitudes

S OCIAL attitudes in the 'thirties and early 'forties were interesting and were only changed a little by the communal nature of war. There was still a noticeable carry-over among our elders of an almost servile Victorian attitude to class and one's place in society. The implication being that if you were born into one class you were destined to remain in it and that to seek to change would be presumptuous and likely to fail. People who happened to live in the country in anything bigger than a farm cottage were spoken of almost in hushed tones as 'County' people, as if they were a race apart. Terms like 'High class butcher' would be found on shop fronts; and expressions like 'select' and 'exclusive' were common parlance.

In fact, no one among friends of my own age had any concept of 'class' as such, thank Heaven; it seemed an attitude of mind, to which one could easily become captive, rather than a reality. We just reacted to people according to what sort of person they were, kind and considerate, rude or selfish, rather than conforming to any idea of social class. It didn't matter what our friend's father was or did, or where they lived. It was whether they were a good friend or not that was important. This not so much broke down barriers as failed to accept them, so that we could enjoy each other's company without preconceived notions.

We were living with ingrained social attitudes of the 'thirties, where people on housing estates for instance would have a strong sense of 'respectability' and of morality too. Quite properly, they kept their gardens neat, their windows washed, and polished the brass on the front door, but could get quite sniffy about unkempt gardens or wrecks of old bikes or cars at someone else's house. They therefore virtually created a class structure within their own assumed social group. Yet in spite of this each others' privacy would always be respected, and help would readily be offered to anyone who needed it - if there was a funeral then curtains all down the street would be closed as a mark of respect as it passed by. It was assumed that the higher up the social scale one looked, the better the example of behaviour which would be seen, and it was a source of dismay and disappointment if this was not always found to be the case, due to tales of levity in high places. In short, Puritanism remained a potent governor of social attitudes, and for someone to say of an action or an attitude 'I reckon nowt of it' was to damn it to all eternity!

It was not at all surprising therefore, at the 'Victory in Europe' celebrations in May 1945, when carefully stored 'rations' were brought forth for a giant communal party round a bonfire, that people who had lived near each other for twenty years, with unspoken barriers between them, met and talked socially almost for the first time. And when wines and spirits were seen in public too, outside the home or the proper 'Public house', it seemed scandalous to some. Attempts to start a 'Residents Association' to foster this sudden egalitarianism were thus almost bound to flounder. People weren't unfriendly, it just wasn't their way. I have since learned that Holme Slack has a very active Residents Association at present, so clearly social attitudes have changed for the better since the 1930s and '40s.

My mother strongly disapproved of my father taking me to the Palace Theatre, to which I have referred, however good and famous the act, because Music Halls still had the taint of being 'common'. I was allowed to visit the Albert Snooker Hall on Garstang Road so long as we played only billiards and not snooker, because billiards was thought to be more socially acceptable. But parents must do what they think is right at the time as they see it, and best for their children, so I really argue with that; their attitudes were conditioned by their own experience and their way of life.

There were parts of Preston like East Cliff above Avenham Park, which had big houses, like those in Latham Street, Porter Street and particularly in Winckley Square, where the solicitors worked; and houses in Starkie Street, in Ribblesdale Place, in Penwortham, Broughton and Ashton which were thought to be rather 'up market'. But in fact they were merely inhabited by those who had worked hard in business or commerce and had earned their environment, and were just nice people who would have been very embarrassed to be told they were the 'élite' of the town. They would have wondered how on earth to live up to such a title!

If a person worked at the County Offices, he or she was considered to be very much on the ladder of success, since Preston was, and still is, the administrative centre of the County, and wears its position with pride.

As a teenager, I felt very conscious, when I went to the Youth Club which was held in our dear old Deepdale Council School, or played

Badminton at St. James's, that everyone seemed completely at ease, and seemed to say all the right things, often wittily, in each circumstance. Having only just got over an embarrassing stutter myself, I used to wonder if I would ever feel comfortable in such a group, particularly with girls. But when my father said 'Just relax, and keep trying – it's all part of growing up – it comes with the spots; and the others almost certainly feel the same if they'd admit it'. He removed a barrier, and I was forever grateful to him for that. So once I overcame that initial and painful shyness I found I was able to enjoy people's company in all parts of the area, be welcomed into their houses and associations quite naturally, and just to be myself. I have since in the course of my duties met and talked with the highest in the land and found the same unassuming friendliness; in fact in many cases the higher they were, the nicer they were, for they had probably achieved their aspirations and were relaxed.

CHAPTER TEN

# Evening Classes

I HAVE mentioned evening classes. These became almost a way of life during the winter. There was no 'day release' of apprentices to study at college as there is now, so if we had a full time day job we had to go to 'night school'. My main recollection of The Harris Institute Technical College was of its sheer competence. We were attending purely voluntarily, and probably paying for it too; though I was lucky, my results at Deepdale Modern School had earned me a free scholarship, and subsequent year's efforts continued this year to year. So even though we didn't have to attend or even pay, Mr Naylor the Principal would still stand near the top of the stairs and give us a ticking off if we were late! He took the view that if we were going to do it at all - we should do it properly.

Every one of the teachers we had were experts in their subjects and taught them well. The name of Mr Wrigley stands out particularly in my mind. He transmitted such an enthusiasm for engineering, made it sound so interesting and so worth doing, and we did such good experiments in the lab, that what could easily have been a long chore became a pleasure to us all. His success rate among his students was phenomenal. And it wasn't just theory. He was a proven engineer passing on his hard won knowledge.

I think it was there that a rather spectacular accident occurred. One of the enormous flywheels, mounted on the fast rotating shaft of a big gas engine in the basement laboratory, broke loose. With tremendous momentum it trundled across the floor, demolished one brick wall, went right across a classroom, which fortunately was empty, and buried itself in the far wall without harm to anyone.

For many of us the course we took was the Ordinary National Certificate lasting three years of winter classes. Then there were two further years for the Higher National Certificate. To become a Graduate of the

72

*Preston Harris Institute Technical College
as I knew it.*

Institution of Mechanical Engineers which was our coveted aim, we then had to do a further year of Industrial Administration. As I mentioned earlier, I chose also to take endorsement subjects in Theory of Structures – that Meccano set still influencing my thinking, and Electrical Engineering.

Then again responding to Fred Lang's view that there was more to life than engineering, I attended for a further year and studied English Literature, and got a teacher who made the language positively sing as she read passages from Thomas Gray, Shakespeare, Wordsworth and Dickens to us; and not least, in a wholly authentic accent, the works of the Lancashire poets. She even strayed into Scottish literature and introduced us to the passionate and loving poems of Robert Burns, and the splendour of Sir Walter Scott, so that I was a total convert to their genius long before I made my home in their magnificent Scottish Border country. I think that often it is only necessary for a discerning teacher to introduce a receptive pupil to the joys of great literature and music. It need not always be taught in detail – it can often speak well enough for itself. The student then has the pleasure of discovering and liking it for his own reasons, and in his own way. That is what she did. I believe Fred Lang knew that too. You have only to glance at a copy of some of the great East Lancashire dialect poems of Samuel Laycock, with his 'Welcome Bonny Brid', or Edwin Waugh's 'Come whoam to thi childer an' me', for them to scream the anguish of a father trying to bring up his family during the great Cotton Famine of the nineteenth century; or trudging around in search of honest work which wasn't to be had. Those poems paint the picture well enough, they have no need of further explanation, other than the background fact that it was the disruption of supplies of cotton during the American Civil War which brought the famine, and devastated Lancashire Mill Towns which were wholly dependent on it. If I seem preoccupied with matters of so long ago, it was because my granny was born during that period and told me harrowing tales of those times, passed on by her mother; so I felt I had an historic link with the events, if only by hearsay. If Preston escaped the very worst of those days it was because it had some other industry and could count itself fortunate indeed, though cotton was still its main product. I am proud to have played a part in persuading the editor of the *Oldham Chronicle*, some years ago, to reissue their splendid book of poems called *A Lancashire Miscellany* by James Bennett, which had gone out of print; and which in dialect and other poems by those and other authors, portrayed the distress, streaked with the pure comical fun and optimistic humour, of the Lancashire of the cotton towns when 'times were bad'.

So there was far more to Preston Technical College in Corporation Street than just technical studies; it catered for both vocation and leisure, it widened our horizons, brightened our winters, and did it very well indeed.

Sometimes after night school, if I was on the night shift, I would call at a chip shop in Marsh Lane on the way to work and take in 14 three pennorths of chips for my workmates. It was a standing order, with money from a 'chip kitty' we kept, and my books would smell of chips for days afterwards! Those seven winters from 1943 to 1950 at 'The Tech Coll' were very fruitful and the teaching staff well earned their rewards – what a great place that was! I have felt the benefit of those studies time and time again ever since.

CHAPTER ELEVEN

# Memories of Buildings, Markets and Shops in Preston

W ITH ALL the family at home it wasn't always possible to do the vast amounts of night school homework we were given. So I would get onto a bus and go to the reading room of the Harris Library Museum and Art Gallery. When I had finished my assignment and got it out of the way I would then take the chance to have a good look round the building. I well remember the controversy surrounding the price paid by the Art Gallery for a painting 'Pauline in the Yellow Dress' by a man called Gunn. It caused a furore and attracted huge numbers of extra visitors, which was probably no bad thing! I must say I liked it, it was bright, very well done, and different. But my favourite painting in that gallery, to which I returned time and again and would buy tomorrow if I could afford it, was Charles Spencelayh's 'Why War?'. I thought it was brilliant, not only in its extraordinary detail of everything in the room, but also for the look in the old man's eyes as he realised, in 1939, that we were again to be plunged into war, when he thought his efforts in the previous one had helped to win lasting peace.

I had always had a soft spot for the library since the time, as a boy of twelve, I had answered a frantic call for a copy of 'Treasure Island' for an exhibition of kids' books they were putting on. I had lent them mine and got the princely some of two and sixpence for my trouble, and a letter from the Chief Librarian himself, no less! When my mountaineering and photographic guru W. A. Poucher published a new book on moun-

*I used to like to visit the Harris Library Museum and Art Gallery.*

tain photography, such as 'Lakeland through the Lens' Fred Lang would usually know about it, (I sometimes think that lad had a hot-line to Heaven!), and he would tell me. I would then make a special journey to town to look at it in the Reference Library because I could be sure they too would know of it and would have obtained a copy.

I used to watch the long Foucault's Pendulum as it swung in the same plane all day while the earth revolved under it, and wonder how the devil anybody had got up to that high lantern to fasten it on! The museum with its Roman relics dug up in Ribchester, its glazed pottery and its old fashioned clothing was always interesting.

My elder sister Doreen was later to bequeath to that museum, in her Will in 1965, the ancient Town Cryer's bell of 18th Century Preston, which may have belonged to an even earlier period. About fourteen inches high with a black carrying handle and brass bell it had stood on the hall table at home through generations of my family. It was always kept brightly polished, though its clapper was rather ineffective and probably not the original, but it was a treasured family heirloom worthy of being shown in the town of our birth. On one occasion when a local character called Bill Walmsley announced he was going to compete in the national 'Town Crier' contest, my mother offered him the use of the bell, since he was the first incumbent of that post that we knew of this century. But he declined with thanks, saying that the bell was too valuable to risk damaging it.

*I regretted the passing of the old Town Hall with its fine Victorian Gothic spire.*
Photo Harry Cottam

*Fishergate, c.1952, the Miller Arcade is on the right. This is a view of Preston which,*
*thankfully, has changed little in the last forty years.*
Photo Harry Cottam

I liked the paintings of old Preston that lined the stairs of the library building; and I still have a large copy print of a painting by R H Bentham of the Harris building seen from Friargate in the late 18th century, such as you could buy at the counter. I always regretted the way that such a fine building ended so abruptly at a high wall fronting the market square and wished the steps could have continued down to make a grander entrance.

Apart then from being able to do my homework, with plenty of room to spread my papers out on those large reading room tables, I was able to spend many happy hours in that splendid building. With the Sessions Hall and the old Town Hall before it burned down, an event I well remember, it formed the finest group of buildings in the town.

I regretted the passing of the old Town Hall with its fine Victorian Gothic Spire, and its richly ornate Guild Hall which was reached by an impressive staircase and overlooked Fishergate. It's a pity that the soothsayer, whom Caesar ignored to his cost, didn't look further into the future and warn the worthies of Preston too, for it was on the Ides of March, 15 March 1947 that it burned down! I remember too that not all of it was destroyed, the part overlooking the Market Place was saved, but Preston lost one of its most cherished and recognisable landmarks that night.

*The Park Hotel, seen from Miller Park. In my imagination it was the magnificent 'Chateau Frontenac' of Quebec.*

Another building in Preston which I much admired was the former 'Park Hotel' standing prominently above that most beautiful of Preston's parks – Miller Park. It was a tribute to my history teacher at Deepdale Modern, whose vivid account of the storming of the sea cliffs at Quebec by General James Wolfe, achieving victory in death on the plains of Abraham in 1759, that the Park Hotel was for ever after, in my imagination, the magnificent 'Chateau Frontenac', which stood proudly above those Heights of Abraham. It is marvellous how the lessons of great teachers like that can bear delicious fruit for so long afterwards!

I used also to imagine, as a small boy, the elegant ladies with long dresses, bustles, big hats and parasols, strolling along the top promenade of Miller Park or Avenham Walk on the arm of a dignified gentleman sporting a moustache, top hat and frock coat. Those were the days when they knew how to enjoy their leisure, instead of rushing about too busy to think of strolling. And to think it wasn't all that long ago – my own parents were Victorians.

We were also very proud of the fact that the beautiful Maudland spire of St. Walburg's was then the third highest building in Britain. But 1930s style architecture was also making itself felt, particularly in the Ritz Cinema and in the fine Co-op building in Ormskirk Road, in the Labour Exchange, and in the Municipal Buildings. The big hotels were the Bull and Royal in Church Street where I attended several glittering events, and the Victoria and Station Hotel on the north side of Fishergate overlooking the railway. But there were several other very good hotels down Fishergate Hill too.

It was possible in those days to drive directly from the 'Old Prison' at the end of Deepdale Road right down Church Street and Fishergate, and beyond down to Broadgate or up Penwortham Hill. I think Lune Street was possibly one way only down to Friargate, but then you could

*Lune Street and the splendid Public Hall, of which only the façade remains today.*
Photo Harry Cottam.

79

turn either way. There just wasn't the need for much control because there wasn't a lot of traffic. I can think of few, if any, other one way streets in the town. Access to all parts was very easy and parking was seldom a problem, especially when the covered market was free for that purpose. It was there that a silly little thing happened. My sister had an old Ford Eight, and once when we were returning to it after dark, from a family visit to the Hippodrome, she opened the door and we all piled in, but then her other key, for the ignition, wouldn't fit. She fiddled with it for a long time before one of us, looking round more closely, realised that we were in the wrong car, and ours was the one next to it!

However, on Bank Holidays, Blackpool Road could experience traffic jams, and there was an active programme of dual carriageway building with special cycle tracks at the side.

The market days used to fascinate me, there was always such a bustle of activity on the open market in front of the Harris building. I thought as a lad that I could probably buy anything there, there seemed such a variety. It was on that market place on Victory-in-Europe night in 1945, when every square inch was full of cheering happy crowds in carnival mood, that I saw a stupid act of hooliganism when a bunch of morons, standing on top of the air raid shelters lining the edge of the square, threw lighted fireworks into the crowd and badly burned a small girl who a moment before had been happily enjoying the fun. When they

*Every year my father, seen her on the left, proudly attended the Remembrance Day Parade at the Cenotaph.*

saw what they had done they just ran away. I wonder what sort of adults they became?

I also liked the old fish market building behind the Post Office and the covered market, not only for its draughty echoing spaciousness, and its splendid Victorian ironwork, but because there was a baked potato cart with a glowing fire and much ornate metal on the oven, and it was lovely to buy one of his steaming hot potatoes on a cold wintry day, after the theatre or cinema.

My father was always proud to attend the annual Remembrance Day parade at the impressive Cenotaph in the Market Square. He would put on his Great War medals and join his fellow members of the Border Regiment, and those of other Regiments and Services in remembering fallen comrades. When he died I am sure he would have been proud to know that one of the nicest wreaths at his funeral, sent especially and thoughtfully to that remote church in the Chilterns, was from the Preston branch of his beloved Border Regiment.

Well known shops in Preston in my youth were Mears, a veritable treasure house of toys; Booths, which I have already mentioned; Gooby's, in Church Street, which was a great favourite with the ladies; and the lovely shops of the Miller Arcade like Forshaws flower shop, Sharps drapers and leather goods, and the little cigarette kiosk in the middle which was the place for friends and sweethearts to rendezvous. There was a branch of Burtons, the gents outfitters, in Fishergate and they had a poster which said 'Let Burtons Dress You!' to which some wag had added, 'No thanks, I can dress myself - I'm a big boy now!'

There was a large shop called Wilding's, no relation, which sold household and bathroom accessories. There was also a stamp shop in Corporation Street near Fishergate which supplied me with stamps for my ever growing collection. There were also several family-owned shops like Merigold's for toys, near the New Victoria Cinema; Jamiesons shoes; Turners shoes; Forsyth's jewellers; and Halewoods, a treasure-trove of all kinds of books. I liked the technical stores on Friargate Hill because they sold things like set squares, slide rules, technical books, graph paper and drawing instruments, and I felt quite the proper little scientist when I came out proudly clutching those items to my chest and looking forward to using them at night school!

The church of St. James in Avenham Lane was a fine building, with an impressive entrance porch. It seems such a pity that like St. Marks in Preston, falling attendances or the expense of upkeep led to its closure. It became our family church when my mother joined the Mother's Union there in which some of her friends were members; and Doreen, Norman and I joined their Badminton club. There was a remarkable young chorister called Joseph Ward who had a fine voice, quite the equal of the more famous Ernest Lough in his singing of 'Oh for the

*The Church of St. James in Avenham Lane.*
Photo by Harry Cottam

*St. James had a fine entrance porch.*

82

*This view of Avenham streets now demolished is taken from Avenham Flats.*
Photo by Harry Cottam

*Fylde Road had an 'Ironduke' street toilet.*
Photo Harry Cottam

83

Wings of a Dove'. The vicar, the Reverend Albert Smith gave him every encouragement in allowing him to sing solos, and the church would be full as people came along to hear the wonderful soaring notes of that fine young singer.

## CHAPTER TWELVE

# Scouting in Preston

M ANY OF my friends at school were in the Scouts, and I had once been a Wolf Cub, so in early 1942 I joined too. Lord Baden Powell, the founder of the movement, had died only the year before, and Scouting was immensely strong in Preston.

I joined St. Philip's Troop in Kent Street off St. George's Road. I can't think why, unless I knew someone who was in it, but I'd heard it was very good and it was. It was a good start if a little boisterous for a wee lad, required to support several large kids on my back during one game, or run the gauntlet of many more in 'British Bulldogs', or take part in what I was told was the manly art of boxing. But it was fun - we had good Scouters and Patrol leaders and the minister, a wise and kindly man, used to come in at the end to give us a little chat, and perhaps a thought to go home with, and end the meeting with prayers.

It was normal in all such church groups to hold periodic Sunday morning church parades. But it was the hymns they sang which I particularly liked - good rousing singable hymns; none of your half hearted self conscious murmur with that congregation! Neither were the tunes of the complicated type outside your vocal range, that you are only beginning to get the hang of when the hymn ends. They sang because they meant it, with an evangelical fervour which quite won me over! I took to going there on a Sunday evening too, even though it was a long way from home. I had for so long been a member of St. Oswald's church choir as a boy that I was fond of a good sing, but had never encountered anything quite like St. Philip's.

It was with real regret therefore that I allowed myself to be talked into joining other boys in a new breakaway church Scout group called St. Aidan's. I didn't really like the odd uniform they wore, and at a Scout camp a chap turned up in gaiters, buckled shoes, a frock coat and a tall hat with what I can only describe as 'flying buttresses' to support the crown, and announced that he was the new bishop of this very nonconformist schism. I really felt that this was all going a bit too far; and coupled with the fact that one of the kids had taken to throwing axes around, I decided it was time to go. If the church and the troop still exist then good luck to them but they made rather an eccentric start!

Around this time, late 1942, a chap I knew, Bob Nuttall, had decided to start a Scout group that was to become the 57th Preston St. Oswald's. It would meet in Croft's brickworks hall by the big chimney half way along Holme Slack Lane, 100 yards from home. So I went along and found to my great pleasure that so did many of the local lads including our next door neighbour Dennis Finney, Tom's younger brother; Dennis Dunnigan; a lad called Beardsworth and many other old school friends.

Because I was one of the few who had already been a Scout I was appointed the first Patrol Leader of the Eagle Patrol, and very soon after, Dennis Finney became my Second, and was a tower of strength as we helped build up the patrol and the troop in numbers and in quality.

Bob Nuttall, with an ecumenical sense ahead of his time, arranged for us to join the St. Teresa's Troop of the Catholic College in a 'harvesting camp' at Weeton near Blackpool. We worked on nearby farms and picked up potatoes after the lifting machine, and stacked stooks of corn. This was a good move because we were in contact with a well established group and we made many friends and learned a lot from them. But I felt a great sense of injustice when I thought I had done my bit for the moment and was 'resting on my laurels' - or at least on my pitchfork, when the farmer came in to sight and said 'Look at yon - he's supposed to be t'Gaffer an' he looks as if he's t'laziest beggar of th'lot of 'em!' I don't think I put my pitchfork down for two hours after that; and I've been suspicious of people who generalise from the particular ever since! I think we can learn something from every single experience of our lives.

St. Oswald's went from strength to strength and soon we had our own Scout band with side kettle drums, bugles, and a big bass drum played by Bill Gradwell, Bob's Troop Leader. The band was led by the Union Jack and our own shiny new troop flag with the Scout badge and troop name emblazoned on it, and we held frequent church parades to the relatively new St. Oswald's church.

It is amazing to realise now that we thought nothing then of parading slowly along the main Blackpool Road taking up half its width for several hundred yards! With today's traffic the Police would have a fit!

St. Oswald's first vicar, the Reverend Taplin, a jovial man whom the young kids adored, had recently left. He had been replaced by the devout but much more austere, T. Cyril Batten, whose manner matched the severity of the church interior; the very new modern design of which seemed a little cheerless after the familiarity of St. Philip's. But I learned to appreciate St. Oswald's church for its simple dignity, and its minister for his direct, no frills approach to Christianity. He gave our emerging Scout troop a tremendous lot of help and support in its early days. It was he who instigated the honourable custom in our parish of draping our two flags over the altar during parade services, a gesture which made us very proud.

*We went camping and wore our wide-brimmed hats.*

We had what we called 'Scouting outings'. We camped and played 'wide games' over large tracts of country. We played at stalking, building bivouac shelters from fallen branches and leaves, and lighting camp fires. We would have a 'sausage sizzle' or roast potatoes and kebabs on the open fire, and drink gallons of cocoa. We carried Scout staffs, about five feet long and marked in feet and inches so we could measure the height of things - whatever use that was! There were about two dozen of us - quite a decent sized troop. The uniform consisted of polished shoes; long socks with a garter tab protruding; brown shorts; khaki shirts; a red neckerchief with a white rim, which my mother used to iron carefully before each meeting; and that funny wide brimmed, indented hat that made us look like miniature Canadian mounted police.

There had been a time earlier when I was a Cub, Marjorie was a Brownie, Norman was a Scout, all in St. Jude's, and Doreen was a Guide in the Christ Church Company. Church parades were sheer hell for my mother getting us all off on time and scrubbed until we were squeaky clean with everything smart & pressed!

Bill Gradwell lived in Deepdale Mill Street and once, when I went to call on him, his mother said 'He's gone camping'. 'Funny!' I thought, 'he didn't say anything to us!' Just then he turned up and it transpired that 'to go camping' meant to go visiting friends. It was a Lancashire term I hadn't heard before. But I heard some more shortly afterwards. Bill used to play the carillon of bells at the nearby St. Luke's church. They were played from a keyboard and popular hymns could be played to summon the faithful to church. This being his practice night, Bill asked the verger if I might be allowed to play them. 'Tha con if tha wants' he said, 'but if tha mekks a mistake tha'll be heeard for a mile around, so think on!' So after a bit of practice I jokingly turned to Bill and said 'Now for an encore I'll play Beethoven's Fifth Symphony' to which the verger replied 'If tha con do that lad - I reckon tha con plait custard!' I doubt if there's a sound in the world that falls sweeter on the ear of a Lancastrian than the humour and sound of his native tongue, especially when he's been away for a long time.

So the Scout troop flourished, we visited St. Peter's troop and they came to us. Our lads were working hard for their badge awards and there were new investitures every month.

But then we hit problems. Bob Nuttall was called up for the army, because even toward the end of the war anyone who was not engaged in the sort of 'reserved occupation' that we were at English Electric, was liable to be required for the Forces; and Bill Gradwell too had to depart. That left us Scouterless. We patrol leaders were too young, and though Bob came along when he could, as did other Scouters serving in the army locally, there was no continuity. When Crofts then announced that they needed their hut back it was the last straw. We met for a time in a big bell tent in our garden but we could no longer obtain insurance without a qualified leader. So after about only four years of enjoyable existence, the 57th Preston St. Oswald's Scout Troop had to be suspended in early 1946. I have heard since that it has been re-formed, in which case I wish it well - they inherit a short but proud tradition.

At that time in Preston there were very many Scout troops, though not as many as 57 because several had folded. But their numbers were retained in case they could be reformed as has happened with St. Oswald's.

St. Peter's was a large and active troop, so was 5th Preston St. Cuthbert's, with my school chum Geoff Halsall. 9th Preston Emmanuel was into everything worthwhile with the redoubtable Fred Lang and Frank Cocking among its members. Its leader was Frank Shufflebottom who had been an army cook and could turn a campfire meal into a banquet. St. Thomas's Scouts were a large troop with my other school friends, 'Ats' Bennell and Ronnie Flitcroft, taking a particularly active part in the district Scout gang shows that were put on. St. Thomas's Scout leader, Bill Fazackerly, was known and respected throughout the district as 'Faz'. He had joined the movement as long ago as 1925.

It was 'Faz' who would march out very upright and in immaculate uniform in front of long and impressive processions of Scout troops for district church parades. Each group would be led by its troop, Union Jack flags, and drum and bugle bands. The Guide companies with their own flags and the Brownies and Cubs would all be in the parade too, down Lancaster Road from the assembly point under the covered market, to the Parish Church of St. John in Church Street.

I have had the honour of taking part in, or attending, several big ceremonial events since then, often with Royalty present. But I still rate those District Scout Church Parades as the most moving. St. John's had its balcony in those days, and I can recall, as if it were yesterday, watching from that vantage point the colour parties, representing each troop and company, marching proudly up the aisle to the marvellous swell of the great organ, as it played 'Proudly Gleams our Banner Pointing to the Sky'. Each of dozens of flags would then be laid reverently on the altar by the Reverend Gordon Fallows, Vicar of Preston. We would always sing the hymn 'I Vow to Thee My Country'; and the whole event would be an inspiring and memorable demonstration of the strength and dedication of one of the many youth organisations in Preston in those days.

By this time I had joined a Rover Scout Crew for those over 17 years old. This was 51st Preston, sponsored by the Toc H. organisation. We wore their black neckerchief, with the Cross of Lorraine embroidered in gold on it, to signify that organisation's connection with the Flanders battlefields of the First World War.

We had been members of various Scout Troops so it was nice for good friends like Geoff Halsall and Dennis West, Tony Marks, Ian Som-

*Some members of 1st Broughton Scout Troop, 1952.*
Photo the author

89

merville, Eric Grime, Frank Moss and Tom Gregson - a printer in Preston, who led the Crew at that time - to meet together and take part in corporate activities. We met over a shop in Friargate and the younger ones formed a very enjoyable Rover/Ranger group with girls of our own age, who would come hiking with us. The Rangers was the girls' equivalent organisation. We would meet on the Ribble Bus Station in Tithebarn Street, and a typical outing would be to take the bus to Brock, then hike up the valley alongside the river to emerge near Beacon Fell. We might then go on to climb Fairsnape and the valley to the north, where, in an old farm building, we would have our picnic, sometimes up to ten of us. Just to be sociable we'd swap girl friends so that we all got to know each other better. Then we would make our way down Parlick Pike to Chipping, where we would have a great party in the Sun Hotel while we waited for the last bus back to Preston. Bleasedale was a great place for hiking and fell walking and the Higher Brock Cafe near Beacon Fell would do a roaring trade late on a Sunday afternoon when walkers came down from the fells.

Another favourite hiking region was from Chipping along by the Hodder to Whitewell, with a stop for refreshment at the lovely old hotel there, then on to Dunsop Bridge and perhaps Slaidburn, from where we would get the bus home. Even now, whenever I hear that most evocative of all bird sounds, the call of the curlew, my mind goes back to those enjoyable walks with the Rovers and Rangers over the Slaidburn moors - great fun and happy memories of those summer Sundays long ago.

It was in that crew that I first met Tony Marks. His father and mine had shared an interest in motor bikes in a motor-cycling club, and Stan Marks had gone on to build up a large motor-cycle and scooter retail outlet in Lancaster Road, Preston. Although I had a motor bike too, an old 350cc 1937 John Marston Special Sunbeam, I'd have given my eye teeth to have one of the 'Matchless' or the 350cc AJS demonstration bikes with 'Tele-draulic' suspension that Tony got to ride in those days in 1948!

Now another Scout group that was very active and enterprising in the area was 1st Broughton. Tony ran the seniors' section but said he needed help with it because it was getting a bit large. So I agreed to join him as Assistant Scoutmaster Seniors, the section for the 15-17 year olds. In fact this was a bit hopeful considering I was only 20 myself! But we had fun. He was a mine of good ideas for Scouting activities and I used to watch him write up the troop log in an enormous book-keeping ledger every week. Like most young men about that age we would hold long philosophical discussions on matters of religion, and get terribly serious about 'Why we were here on earth', 'what did we want to do with our lives' etc. - again, all part of growing up I suppose, but useful as sounding boards for half-formed attitudes and ideas.

*1st Broughton Senior Scouts, c.1950.*

Many years later there was an amusing incident when, as a Royal Naval Chaplain, he invited my wife and me aboard his ship, the huge aircraft carrier *Bulwark.* My wife was within a few weeks of the birth of our first child, and we were posed with the question 'How does she get down a vertical companionway ladder in that condition?' His answer came: 'Slowly, carefully, and backwards at arm's length!'

Some time afterwards I was reminded of how those conversations we held in Broughton Scout hut, and during long breezy walks along the promenade at Blackpool, had come to fruition many miles away and years later. I had returned his hospitality by inviting him to come to preach at the Royal Air Force College, Cranwell, where I was on the Staff. The Commandant was present, as were my colleagues, and the church was full. As I listened to his sermon (no 'hangman' this time!) I couldn't help reflecting how both of us had realised our fondest wish. He, in his calling to the Church, was by now a Chaplain to the Queen; while I, with my wish to be among aeroplanes, was a Senior Officer running the Aircraft Design Squadron at the very Mecca of the Royal Air Force. And this was the outcome of hopes and aspirations spoken of so long ago in Preston. Happiness and fulfilment don't often come to you, you have to go out and make them happen.

There were some great lads in 1st Broughton Seniors, later to become Rover Scouts: the Robinson brothers Derek and Brian, Alan Law, John Wreford, Roger Bell, master of long winded 'shaggy dog' stories. There

91

was Mike Higginson, David Thorn, Peter Brooks, Bill Denitz, Tony 'Tusker' Pearson, Brian Spicer, Dai Pritchard, and many more. Frank Goodenough was the hardworking Scoutmaster who also organised our Saturday evening dances in the village hall. 'Doc' Livingstone was the ever smiling and tolerant group Scoutmaster, and Mr Pugh was the totally imperturbable Rover Scout Leader.

Roger Bell's ability to make a short story long was never better demonstrated than when we all went to Kandersteg in Switzerland just after the war. In a park in Interlaken, while we gazed up at the great Eiger and Jungfrau mountains, he told a story that lasted the better part of half an hour and whose final punch line, would you believe, was 'Ogle bloggle'!

Later that week Tony and I got a real ticking off from W. C. Park, who was in charge of the party, and who of course was nicknamed 'Flush'. He had learned that we had taken a ride in what was little more than a low sided soap box, suspended from a cable hundreds of feet above the valley floor, to reach the top of a mountain, when the box was supposed to be used only for the transport of food supplies to an army outpost at the summit.

Once, when we were shopping in Kandersteg, an elderly lady behind the counter seemed to be moving around busily and working very efficiently, and Tony complimented her on this. Her reply in broken English became a catchphrase with us if ever a compliment came our way; - 'Always,' she said, 'I have try to do my possible!'

On that same trip, Tony and I visited Milan where we met an Italian ex-prisoner of war who had spent some time in a camp very like that for Italians on Moor Park in Preston. He was so grateful for his kind treatment - they were allowed out in overalls with a big brown spot on the back - that he showed us round La Scala Opera House, took us to see Da Vinci's 'Last supper', and invited us back for tea with his family.

1st Broughton Scouts was a group which always seemed to do interesting and worthwhile things. We would camp at Great Tower above Windermere and learn the ways of the forest from Captain Parker, the Warden. We would take a boat out on the lake, practice woodcraft, have camp fire sing-songs and walk the fells.

It was nice just to be there, letting the magic of the Lake District weave its spell on us.

At Broughton, behind the vicarage, there was a custom-built, well equipped Scout hut. Each Patrol had its own corner, and there was a room at either end for senior Scouts and Cubs. Both the Scout troop and the Cub pack were large, and the Troop had shown the high standards they set by winning the Scorton Cup more than once at the Scorton Cycle Rally.

This was an annual gathering of Scouts from all parts of Lancashire at which Preston was always well represented. The rule was that you should cycle with your kit to the event at the little village just north of Garstang. On arrival, each troop would be allotted a camp site on a nearby farm. In the evening a grand impromptu concert would be held in the village hall on the Saturday of the weekend event, to which each troop was asked to contribute a turn. I remember I found myself reciting 'The Lion and Albert' in my best imitation of Stanley Holloway. Frank Goodenough, no mean baritone, sang a song but forgot the words, so he sang the same verse twice for good measure!

On the Sunday morning everyone donned his best uniform for the formal inspection by the County Commissioner, Colonel Ord, accompanied by his District Commissioner, J. Dodds Drummond - now there was a name with a ring to it! The Scorton Cup would be awarded for the best camp site, pitching of tents, woodcraft gadgets, turn out of the patrol members and so on. Then while everyone still looked smart there would be a big church parade to the village church. After lunch there was the Great Football Match with around fifty Scouts on each side and only one ball. The result was inclined to be somewhat inconclusive, and I would imagine that something like that rough house would be all the training the SAS would need in future!

I have mentioned church parades several times. It is merely because almost every Scout troop and Guide company in Preston was sponsored and given premises by one of the churches, so loyalty was due and given. The church played a very big part in the life of Preston at that time; hence the many references to Saints in this narrative, which in places have made it read like a roll call of the Heavenly Host! Congregations in many of the churches would be large, and their attendant youth and adult organisations were very active, as witness the Whitsuntide processions.

I seem to recall that only one or two other places, Manchester I believe among them, held Whitsuntide processions as Preston did. There would be processions by the Church of England churches, another one for the Catholic churches, one for the so called 'Nonconformist' churches - the Methodists, Baptists, and Wesleyans - and one for the Orangemen.

Each church group would be preceded by a huge embroidered banner about ten feet square with a religious motif and the name of the church on it, and it would be supported at each side by poles, which men would wear in holsters below waist level, hung from straps round the neck. If the wind caught the banner it would act like a sail, and the men would have to stagger to keep it upright and straight. To assist them there would be cords and coloured ribbons leading from the banner and held by young ladies, beautifully dressed all alike, in dresses made specially for the event. And they weren't just decorative either, for without a timely pull on the cords in a wind all of them were in some danger of taking off!

93

*Sucking an orange, or better still a lemon – loudly!*

Behind them would walk the very young Sunday school children, looking very sweet, the little girls all dressed alike, perhaps as 'Bo Peep', and marshalled by a few mums for those who got tired. Behind them would come the youth groups like the Scouts, the Church Lads Brigade and the Boys Brigade; the Mothers' Union ladies; the men's organisations; and other members of each congregation. The procession, which could be up to a mile long, made a most colourful sight watched by huge crowds, as they passed, usually down Church Street and Fishergate, along Corporation Street, Kendal Street, Friargate, Harris Street, Lancaster Road, North Road, Park Road and back to Church Street.

To accompany the procession there were brass or silver bands at intervals, most of them local, playing familiar marches like 'Colonel Bogey', and marches by Sousa. The trombones would usually be at the front, to be used, it was said, as 'kid shifters', rather like cow catchers on an engine! But actually we knew them as 'thrust and poo backs', because their slides needed room in front to operate without hindrance. Which reminds me of the rather rotten little trick we used to play at band concerts on the parks. We would stand right at the front and gaze in mock rapture at the trumpeters, trombonists and cornet players, while sucking an orange, or better still a lemon - loudly! - it made their upper lips curl, making it difficult for them to play, and we'd be moved on by an attendant!

But in those processions I used to wonder how the walkers managed to keep in step when one band in front was playing one tune, while another just behind was playing a different one, and not even at the same time! It was probably that which led one proud mum to exclaim 'Ee sithee, there's only our Billy in step!' Tony Marks also tells a nice little story of the time he was watching the Catholic procession and suddenly an anxious mother rushed out to her little daughter in the procession and said 'Alice, Owd yer lily up!' and this became his family's expression for 'Keep your pecker up' at less happy moments in their lives.

CHAPTER THIRTEEN

# The Preston Guilds

I FIND it difficult to write much about the Preston Guild Week because I only ever saw part of one of them - and that was in 1952 after I had left Preston. I recall that the previous one was in 1922 before I was born, and that because of the War the Guild due in 1942 was postponed for ten years. I also knew that the Guild had started in 1542 - so it had a long history. But though I was able to return to Preston in 1952 for only one or two events, I can remember them quite clearly. One was the Guild Merchant's Procession and the other was a performance of 'Merrie England' in the lovely Avenham Park.

For the Procession my mother had arranged with the Cavendish Furniture shop to have the use of several chairs on the pavement outside their premises in Friargate, though I very much doubt if they owned the pavement too! At least we had an excellent view of the long procession, which comprised gaily decorated floats showing the products, and in some cases the method of manufacture such as the use of looms, of the many firms and industries in Preston. It was a most colourful, interesting and impressive display.

This, I remember, was in mid-week. That evening at the bottom of the very slope in Avenham Park where we had rolled our 'pace eggs' as children, there was an outstanding performance by local amateurs of Edward German's 'Merrie England', using the slope as a natural tiered amphitheatre. There was excellent singing, staging, and lighting, and the costumes were very colourful indeed. I have seldom seen a performance given with more enthusiasm. And now, whenever I hear its music, my mind goes back to that lovely autumn evening in the town which I still called 'home' long after I had departed.

My parents later wrote to say that the Church processions were even grander and bigger than usual; that the Industrial Exhibition on Moor

95

*Pipe band marching down Friargate past the Hippodrome Theatre, Guild Procession 1952.*
Photo the author

*English Electric Co., Strand Road, Preston, and Warton Exhibit, Guild Procession, 1952.*
Photo the author

Park was fascinating, and that some brave souls had even given a swimming exhibition in the Ribble in September. I hope they knew there was a whirlpool near the Tram Bridge when I was a lad! The Technical College had put on a good exhibition of students' work, and even my old friends in the Preston Scientific Society had chipped in with a good exhibition. The Preston Cecilian Choral Society of 'Messiah' fame had given a concert in my favourite Public Hall; and to end it all there had been a wonderful torchlight procession and carnival. So it seems 'a good time was had by all', and I was there in spirit at least. Hopefully, having had to miss the 1972 Guild as well, I will be able to attend the one in 1992. I would say to anyone who hasn't seen one, that from my own memory, and the enthusiastic reports of those who have seen them, Preston Guilds are well worth going a long way to see.

## CHAPTER FOURTEEN

# Political Preston

POLITICS touched only lightly on my life. I had emerged more as a
Liberal than anything else, largely as a compromise between those
extreme views of the Communist Left, and those of the Conservative
workers I met in the toolroom of English Electric, who were truer blue
Tory than most – blue collar workers perhaps? My mother was a Conservative agent at one time, and one of my very earliest memories was when
she and the Conservative candidate had been campaigning in our region. She invited him in for a cup of tea and he was the tallest man I had
ever seen. His head actually brushed the ceiling light which, to a very
young lad, was somewhere near the clouds! His name, I think, was Kirk-
patrick. My father and the rest of us seldom, if ever, discussed politics.

During the War, Winston Churchill's son, Randolph, was MP for Preston, and I suppose that whatever our politics we all basked in the reflected glory of having the son of the great wartime leader to represent
the town. In a photograph taken of him in army uniform, reviewing a
parade in Preston with A. V. Alexander, First Lord of the Admiralty, and
Capt. E. C. Cobb., Preston's other MP, a 12 year old Albert Evans, now of
New Longton, was shown prominently in the picture at the right hand
side, which prompted the question 'Who are those men with Albert
Evans?'

But of greater interest to us lads was another, later MP for Preston
called Shackleton, son of the famous explorer, Sir Ernest Shackleton.
When not tied up with parliamentary duties, he could be persuaded to
give talks and slide shows on the Antarctic exploits of his illustrious
father. Later, he became well known as Lord Shackleton.

Preston must have been considered a very important constituency to
win, for it attracted famous men to seek to be its representatives in
Parliament.

*Who are those men with Albert Evans? A young Albert Evans on the right shares the picture with (left to right front) Randolph Churchill, M.P. for Preston; A. V. Alexander, First Lord of the Admiralty; Captain E. C. Cobb, Preston's other M.P.; and the mayor, Alderman J. S. Haworth, during Preston's 'warship weekend' in January 1941.*
Photo kindly loaned by Albert Evans

At the end of the war, during the 1945 election, Winston Churchill came to Preston to support the local Tory candidate; and while driving in Blackpool Road just short of Garstang Road, his car broke down. I was standing nearby with my father who gave a hand pushing the car into the nearby Conservative Club, and received a warm smile from the great man for his efforts!

CHAPTER FIFTEEN

# Parks of Preston

I HAVE MENTIONED several of Preston's beautiful parks. The town was, and still is, very fortunate in this respect, and more so than others in terms of the variety, ease of access and maintenance of its parks.

Moor Park was nearest to home so of course whenever we wanted a short walk we would take a paper bag full of broken crusts of bread, and feed the ducks on the duck pond. There would be Mallard, the occasional Moorhen, Tufted ducks, Mute Swans, and Canada Geese. We were warned not to get too close to the swans, particularly in the breeding season, for they would hiss and might attack, and a swan's flapping wings could break a child's limb.

Also on Moor Park was an open air swimming pool, and being a devout coward when it comes to cold water, I would usually choose only the hottest days of summer to swim in it. If it was heated at all it can't have been very effective. But those were the days of 'Biggles', cold baths, Christianity and 'Ripping yarns', when if you took a shower it should be a cold one, and if you took medicine you took it like a man, be it castor oil, Fenning's fever cure or senna pods; if it tasted nasty or was icy cold it must be doing you good they said! I'd have been quite happy to take their word for it!

At the side of Moor Park there was also a very good open air school for children with chest and respiratory ailments, though I should have thought that as traffic increased on the adjacent Blackpool Road, the fumes would not have helped matters. Moor Park was a beautifully big open place with plenty of room for sports and big civic events, and it was around three quarters of a mile from end to end – a fine park which left fond memories of its spaciousness and the field days and fêtes that I went to as a lad. Haslam Park was always very attractive, with lovely flower beds and shrubs. There was a small aviary and even a monkey house and it was a very pleasant place to stroll on a Sunday afternoon. It had been opened in 1910 by our Great Uncle-by-marriage, Alderman William McKune Margerison, so we had more than a passing interest in it.

Ashton park had been the grounds of Ashton house and was also a great wide open space, with a very good pitch-and-putt course. Some of the holes were quite long and wouldn't have been out of place on a full sized course. We had lots of good games on that course - my brother, my father and I.

Waverley Park at the corner of Blackpool Road and New Hall Lane was a great place to watch or to play football on a Saturday morning. I cannot remember much about Frenchwood Park, which was in an area I seldom visited, or Farringdon Park beyond the old cemetery, which I knew only as a destination name on buses.

But the jewels, surely, were those two adjacent parks Avenham and Miller. To walk round that lovely rock garden in Avenham park was a sheer delight, and in such a perfect setting with the grass sloping gently down to the river bank, and those little hidden walks on winding paths through shrubberies and under and over a little stone bridge just inside Miller Park from Avenham. As children we used to chase each other, laughing, round those paths, and play hide and seek, and run up and down those lovely curved steps at the end of Avenham Walk overlooking the Tram Bridge - such happy days!

On the way to it we would almost tiptoe past Winckley Square garden, a quiet retreat of walks, seats, trees and shrubs in an elegant part of town, where the residents, or the professional people who worked in nearby offices could take a lunchtime break in peaceful surroundings.

Next to Avenham was Miller Park, rather more formal but none the less beautiful. If I wanted a single picture of my home town to carry in my memory to distant places, it would be of that view past the central fountain to the Lord Derby statue, and to the splendid Park Hotel above it. I think that Preston Corporation Parks Department did a very good job indeed and the parks always looked nice with little or no vandalism or litter, and were places of which the town could be justly proud.

So to approach Preston from the south by rail, after a long absence, and to pass over the Ribble and see that beautiful view of Miller Park with my beloved 'Chateau Frontenac' standing graciously above it, with Avenham Park beyond, was to make the heart leap with joy, for I knew that I was home.

## CHAPTER SIXTEEN

# Sport in Preston

O F COURSE very many types of sport were available, ranging from the huge Albert Billiards and Snooker Hall in Garstang Road almost opposite English Martyr's church, which I have mentioned, to badminton in church halls. My family learned badminton at St. James's church hall in Knowsley Street off Avenham Lane. My sister Doreen went on to play for her county of residence, Essex; while I played for mine, Wiltshire, as a result of the tuition and practise we got, under that most deceptively clever of players, the Reverend Albert Smith, Vicar of St. James's.

The Preston Grasshoppers were a power in the land of Rugby, and Preston cricket team played at West Cliff above South Meadow Lane. A school friend of mine at Deepdale Modern School was Peter Burgon. He was a great sportsman, a fine swimmer and an excellent cricketer. Peter's skill at sports brought him on one occasion to bowl against a visiting celebrity, the famous West Indian cricketer Learie Constantine, who came to Broughton Cricket Club to play in a charity match. He was later to become Sir Learie, High Commissioner for Trinidad & Tobago. Tom Finney made a guest appearance in his eleven too. Now normally Peter's bowling would have struck terror into any normal club cricketer, but I watched as Learie decided to give the huge crowd its money's worth. He hit seven sixes and lifted one of Peter's less straight ones right out of the ground in a huge strike. The story then went that it landed with a thud on the car of a passing motorist in the main road outside. But when the irate driver learned that it was the Famous Man Himself who had done it, he became rather proud of that hollow on his car roof, and went away quite mollified!

I used to play a bit of cricket too. Ever since I had been allowed to run we had played cricket in 'the circle' at the crossing of Rose Lane and

Lilac Grove at Holme Slack. We used the lamp post as a wicket, and hoped we didn't hit the ball into Ma Hartley's nice garden, because she feared we might trample on her flower beds, and would keep the ball as a deterrent.

But now, years later, the venue was usually Moor Park, with my Drawing Office colleagues, or sometimes we would play on a pitch beyond the tram bridge across the Ribble from Avenham Park. I could bowl the occasional crafty googly and take a few wickets on the right pitch; and I thought I was a fairly useful close fielder until my captain decided I was dispensable, and put me at silly mid on! My batting was atrocious - I used to go in at number eleven and there were those who thought I was a bit too high up the batting order at that! I found out the reason finally - it was that three cricket stumps were wider than a lamp post!

Imagine my apprehension as I went in for one key match; our side had reached the final of the Inter-Office Cup. There were nine of our men down, and we still needed two to win, with only three balls left, when I went in to bat. The first ball I barely kept out of my wicket; the second whizzed past me head high and I could only duck. The third and last one was due. It was now or never. I watched it all the way to the bat and managed to make a good contact. Scenes of glory swam before my eyes as I saw it soar away. I began to run as fast as my little legs could carry me. Then I heard the cheers turn to groans as I was caught at backward square leg.

There was golf at Fulwood - a fine course I believe. But it's a funny thing that I have played golf on dozens of courses throughout Britain, even the old course at St. Andrew's, but never that of the place of my birth. I hope I may be allowed to remedy that sometime!

Most popular however was the amateur football which was played on several of the town's parks. There had even been a 'Dick Kerr's International Ladies Association Football Club' once, who had beaten most other ladies teams in their time.

It was while I was playing football, on the 'back field' behind our houses in Rose Lane Holme Slack as a boy, that I realised that our next door neighbours had a rather extraordinary footballer as a son. I noticed, when I was allowed to join the big boys for a game, that he seemed to put the ball between our two piles of clothes, which were the goal posts, rather more often than most. I was some five years younger and was only playing to make up the numbers, because they got fed up with seeing me standing wistfully by hoping to be asked. But I could see even then that if he could control the ball as well as that on that bumpy uneven meadow, he'd do rather well on a proper pitch. His name was Tom Finney, and it really became a question of 'If Tom was on your side you won, and if he wasn't, you didn't!'

Both our families had children about the same ages and we got on very well as neighbours. If one or other of our mums was making a cup

*I realised that our next door neighbours had a rather extraordinary footballer as their son...*

of tea she would knock on the dividing wall and they would go out for a chat over the garden fence.

Then with the war, Tom went off to the army and his career as a footballer blossomed as all the footballing world knows. Three books written around that time, 'Finney on Football', 'Football Round The World', and 'Instructions to Young Footballers' say it all much better than I could possibly do, and contain some excellent photographs of Tom in action. The footballing press and media were full of his exploits and still are.

There is a very good recent book by Paul Agnew, Sports Editor of the Lancashire Evening Post, called 'Finney - A Football Legend', and a video by writer/director Terence Charnley which add still more to this remarkable story.

So remembering his skill, we weren't at all surprised to hear in 1946 that Tom was playing for England in Northern Ireland, the first of many, many Caps. And he scored a goal too! As recently as November 1989 he was the guest of honour at a Wembley International, all those years after he graced the game. That says a great deal, as does the fact that he was awarded the CBE, appointed a Freeman of his native town, to which he brought such honour, became a JP and is currently President of Preston North End.

Because of the interest I took in his progress I began to attend Preston North End matches regularly after 1946 when he came home. Of course we kids had all heard on the radio how George Mutch had won the FA Cup for Preston in 1938 with his last minute penalty goal. And we had regularly taken advantage of the 'last ten minutes' rule by which children got into the ground free for that period. So we were not uninterested in PNE before 1946. In any case with the ground so near we always knew the score by the cheers or groans which came to us from inside the terraces.

It just needed someone like Tom to turn a passive supporter into an active one. But I didn't realise when I started 'going on the North End' regularly that I was witnessing one of the greatest eras of soccer in Britain generally and in Preston especially. If, perhaps, the club has had its ups and downs since then, it has happened before, and the good times will come again, I'm sure.

During the Finney era, however, PNE were honoured members of the First Division. As well as the sheer joy of watching such consummate skill displayed by Tom - on a proper pitch this time! - I was also privileged to watch such marvellous contemporaries as Raich Carter of Derby; 'Golden Boy' Wilf Mannion of Middlesbrough; Tommy Lawton of Chelsea, a dynamic header even of those heavy leather and often sodden wet balls; England goalkeeper Frank Swift of Manchester, who had such huge hands that he could grasp a football in one of them; Billy Wright of Wolves, winner of 107 England caps; and Stanley Matthews of Stoke and Blackpool. Wasn't it great, in January 1990, to see again that famous trio of Tom Finney, Wilf Mannion and Raich Carter, sitting side by side, as once they had performed magic tricks with a football side by side, at a television tribute to their former colleague Billy Wright, on a 'This is your life' programme! And of course there was an earlier, similar, programme in which Tom himself was the guest of honour. It showed once again, if ever it needed to be shown, that many more than I look back on those footballing days just after the war with marvellous pleasure and nostalgia.

I used to watch PNE play at home one week then go to Bloomfield Road Blackpool the next to watch their team, because fixtures were arranged to allow that. There was one famous period when Blackpool

*Tom Finney attracted a lot of attention from the opposite defences – in this case Elkersley, Horton and Holt of Blackburn Rovers at Deepdale, 1950.*
Photograph courtesy of Tom Finney

had an 'all M' front line who, I think, were Mullen, Mortensen, MacIntosh – formerly of PNE – Munroe and Matthews.

So I saw the whole of the 'Finney versus Matthews' saga, and, if I had to make a judgement with hindsight after all these years, I would acknowledge that of course Matthews was a very good outside right indeed. But that's all he was. He seldom scored a goal, though of course he made plenty, and there was little to suggest he could play anywhere else. Tom, on the other hand, was a natural left footer, and liked playing inside left, as those games at Holme Slack had shown. Yet he played for his country at outside right with marvellous distinction, and did the same in the outside left position. Then for an encore, while playing in a league match at Portsmouth, team captain Bill Shankley switched him in an emergency to centre forward. The commentator, John Macadam, bemoaning the muddy pitch, then went on to describe how Tom, 'astonishing the 42,000 crowd with his innate sense of balance' meandered down the marsh, beating three men in his stride with that deceptively easy swerve, and tapped the ball into goal.

Then, in more colourful language, Macadam went on to describe him with a mixed metaphor: 'an aristocrat of centre forwards, a ballerina of ball players, on a pitch that would have bewitched a duck!' Another commentator described his performance, less embarrassingly, as 'The finest exhibition of centre forward play he'd ever seen or was ever likely to see'. Yet, though Tom had played unofficially at centre forward a few times, this was the first time that the media realised what a remarkably versatile man they were watching.

So it wasn't long before Tom was also gracing the international scene in that position too, and scoring goal after goal in seventy six Internationals. Now who else, before or since could do that? The facts speak for themselves, I can spare Tom's blushes, let his record do the talking.

He played some great matches at Preston too; and I wish, how I wish, I had a copy of that photograph in the Lancashire Evening Football Post of those three Blackburn Rovers players lying on the ground in total disarray as Tom Finney jinked his way past them. He was just like a skier on a slalom course, and left them stranded, as he headed for the town-end goal. That one picture said it all!

I never ever saw Tom be the cause of a foul or ever retaliate, though he was often cruelly slashed down by full backs, sticking out a hopeful and lucky leg, after being driven to distraction all afternoon by his skills.

For with the ball glued to his feet, you'd swear blind he'd go one way as he leaned over and suddenly he'd be away past on the other side. Or he would stop dead, and force the opposing player to make a move, and it would usually be the wrong one. It's a wonder they didn't apply for early retirement!

Before the start of the match and at half time we would be entertained by the excellent Brindle Prize Silver Band. It was led by a shortish stocky young man, who would walk very proudly in front, peak cap, head back, chest out, carrying his drum major's baton about four feet long with a fine silver knob on the top. At intervals he would fling this, twirling, high in the air, to the 'whoooo!' of the crowd, and would catch it with hardly a glance, as if there was no question of him ever missing it, when of course all the kids were hoping he would. But he never did.

In the PNE team at that time were many other skilful and entertaining footballers. Charlie Wayman had an uncanny knack of being in the right place at the right time to score from Tom's crosses. Eddy Quigley, at £26,500 the country's most expensive footballer, could spray passes with pin-point accuracy. Ken Horton scored 22 goals in a season in Preston's promotion year from Division 2, and at any level that wasn't easy. Gooch, the goal keeper, was quite fearless and would dive at an approaching forward's feet, and often sustain shoulder injuries in the process. Angus Morrison scored three goals for Derby in a broadcast match at Preston which PNE won 7-4, and soon after was signed by Preston, where he continued his scoring feats. Joe Walton was a most reliable full back.

Blackburn's clever international Bobby Langton joined PNE at outside left, and played so brilliantly in one particular match that he was applauded off the field, with Tom being the first to congratulate him.

There were the famous Scottish Internationals in Preston's team like Andy Beattie at right back, Bill Shankley, thoughtful and calm at right half, and later came the very enthusiastic and skilful Tommy Docherty.

There was also that other clever little Scot Bobby Beattie, whom I once saw lift a ball over a full back's head into goal from no more than a yard in front of him. Howard Kendal played for Preston at one time. It is surprising how many former PNE players became well known managers later; clearly it was a very good training ground for them.

A 40,000 gate was not uncommon in those heady First Division days. Len Shackleton of Sunderland 'The Clown Prince of Soccer', came along and delighted us with his skills at Preston. Irish International's Peter Doherty of Huddersfield bravely played with a broken arm in plaster. Derek Dooley of Sheffield Wednesday lost his leg after getting an infection from a cut sustained in front of 'Spion Kop'. England captain Stan Hardwick of Middlesbrough was a great attraction. Bert Trautmann who, like our Italian friend in Milan had been a prisoner of war, liked this country so much that he stayed and played goal for Manchester City, and visited frequently. All these names fall off the pen like a roll of honour.

I had been a regular PNE supporter up to 1951 while I lived in Preston; but even after that I managed to see quite a few matches during visits home. So overall I had the privilege of watching PNE for almost 24 seasons.

Now I know Tom Finney will not thank me for heaping still more praise upon him - he's far too modest for that. But one final memory of that period sticks in my mind which to me was a classic - my favourite - and just too good a story to throw onto the scrapheap of fading memories. It was, in short, the cheekiest goal I've ever seen.

It was at Ewood Park Blackburn, a local derby. The ground was full, it held 60,000 people in those days. Tom picked up the ball half way down his right wing, heading towards us as we stood behind the Blackburn goal. Instead of cutting inside as he often did, he continued on down his wing. The opposing full back had long since stopped trying to tackle him, and with the rest of the opposition had moved to the middle in front of goal, to try to cut out what would virtually be a corner as Tom centred.

But he didn't centre, he carried on right to the corner flag to our left. Still they waited, no one daring to tackle him. So he turned and brought it along the by-line. Still no tackle, still no pin-point centre. So further along the by-line, a host of anxious men including the goalkeeper hopping from one leg to the other, dithering and stepping backwards and forwards waiting for the cross. Then suddenly there was no more by-line. Tom was past the nearside post and in front of goal - so he just side footed it in, and 60,000 people, including those very fair Blackburn supporters, roared with laughter!

CHAPTER SEVENTEEN

# Family Matters

I HAVE MENTIONED members of my family several times, and of course my childhood experience of Preston was inextricably linked with theirs. So because as a family we were fortunate indeed to have such good friends in the town, it may be of some interest to them to know what became of us.

Doreen, my elder sister, having worked first in Horrockses then in Hawkins textile firms, as Secretary to their Directors, obtained in 1946, the position of Secretary to the Camp Chief of the Boy Scouts Association, at a lovely country house, set in extensive grounds, called Gilwell Park near Chingford in Essex, where Scouters were trained. This was as a direct result of her work with Christ Church Guides and Rangers over many years in Preston. She was wonderfully happy there for 19 years, and met many interesting and famous people.

For her work at Gilwell she was awarded the Scout Medal of Merit and was presented to the Queen at Windsor Castle. But then, sadly, she contracted cancer in 1964 and died in August 1965 at the age of only 42 years, just eleven days after my wedding which she successfully attended in spite of everything.

Doreen's twin Norman, having briefly sampled a life at sea before the war, used his wartime experience as a radio operator in the RAF to become a Radio Officer in the Merchant Navy after the war. His travels took him to every Mediterranean country, as well as Canada, America, Russia, South Africa and New Zealand. His tales of flying fish, mountainous seas, and having to dodge the knives of villains out to rob him in foreign ports used to enthral us.

When rationing was still with us in 1948, and food was still in short supply, he would bring from Canada, hampers of 4lb. of tea, large jars of jam, 6lb. of sugar, tinned foods, and 6lb. bags of rice - things, and in quantities, that we hadn't seen in nine long years of rationing!

Norman had a wonderfully wicked sense of humour, and many years later when I was proudly showing off my brand new MG Midget to him, I lifted the bonnet and asked him to listen to its beautifully quiet power unit; at which point he cupped his hand behind his ear and shouted 'What did you say? – I can't hear for the noise from this damned engine!' That was typically Norman. Sadly he died of a heart attack in 1967.

Our loving parents never really survived the early deaths of their two elder children; it was too much, and they died within six months of each other in 1969, sadly missed, for we were a happy family. My father was a wise and gentle man. My mother had much more about her than she ever got a chance to show; and the struggle they must have had to bring up two sets of twins, and to give us all a happy childhood during some very lean years cannot have been easy. To say nothing of the fact that she agreed to look after three old people in succession in her house, her father-in-law Thomas Wilding, her mother Elizabeth Cowell, and finally her Aunt Ada, all of whom lived to a great age under her care.

*My elder sister, Doreen, c. 1946. Doreen was awarded the Medal of Merit of the Boy Scouts Association.*

We kids donated a TV set to brighten our parent's winters and a car to brighten their summers and let them continue their beloved motoring. We all popped home to see them whenever we could, and they had more money towards the end than they'd ever had. So we like to think that their sadness was perhaps relieved a little by being able to get out and about into their beloved Lancashire countryside. Mother died in Sharoe Green Hospital aged 76, and my father came south to be near us but died aged 82 a few months later, only weeks after greeting his last grandchild, my son Adrian.

My twin Marjorie decided early on to become a nurse, and worked, studied, and became well qualified at Preston Royal Infirmary, graduating from Nursery Nursing to more general work as a State Registered

*My twin, Marjorie, qualified as a state registered nurse and became a lieutenant in Queen Alexandria's Royal Army Nursing Corps.*

Staff Nurse. In 1950 she was commissioned as a Lieutenant in Queen Alexandra's Royal Army Nursing Corps, serving mainly in southern England, where she met and married James Digby Mackworth, an Army Officer in REME. His duties then took them to Africa, the Continent, and the Far East. They had two children, Amanda and Charles.

Her second marriage was to our dear second cousin John Margerison; which thus re-established her link with Preston, for John's family had an honoured name in the area for their manufacture of White Windsor and other fine soaps. They had contributed significantly to the civic life of Preston on two occasions - 1904-5 and 1909-10 - in the mayoralty of John's grandfather, our great uncle Alderman William McKune Margerison, whom I have already mentioned.

Finally, for what its worth, following the events outlined in this story, I left Preston in 1951 to study for a Master of Science Degree at the College of Aeronautics at Cranfield in Bedfordshire. Then I joined the Vickers Supermarine Aircraft Company, a name that still thrills me, for I was among the aircraft which were the direct descendants of the Spitfires which had played so valiant a role, and helped to save us, during the war. I was based at South Marston in Wiltshire and had five glorious idyllic years doing aircraft research and development; living on the edge of the lovely Cotswold country, going to services in lovely little village churches tucked away in the folds of the hills; attending orchestral concerts in Marlborough College and Salisbury cathedral; and wandering at will round Stonehenge and Avebury. During this time I had the honour of being elected a full member of both the Institution of Mechanical Engineers, and of the Royal Aeronautical Society, and was made a Chartered Engineer.

But in a political climate which needed fewer aircraft the firm had to move to other things; so in 1958, remembering my dream on that bank above Walton-le-Dale, I joined the Royal Air Force as a Flying Officer,

*I lived near the lovely Cotswold country.*
Photo by Doreen Wilding

to continue to be with aircraft, and had eighteen very happy years, mainly teaching Aircraft Structural Theory, and running the Aircraft Design Squadron, and was fortunate in being promoted successively to Flight Lieutenant, Squadron Leader, and finally to Wing Commander. For twelve years I then taught at a College of Technology at Falkirk while living in Peebles in the beautiful and peaceful Scottish Border country. I still keep up my hobby of photography which led me to become President of Falkirk Camera Club, and later a Council member in the Edinburgh Photographic Society, reviving happy memories of the Preston club.

My wife, Julia, is currently studying as a mature student for an MA Honours Degree in History and Sociology at Edinburgh University. Our elder son, Nigel, aged 25, graduated with a 1st class Honours in Physics from the same university and has since been awarded a PhD degree in the subject. Our younger son, Adrian, aged 23, also graduated at Edinburgh University, obtaining a 1st class Honours MA in Politics, and has since taken a second MA at Warwick University, this time in Philosophy. He is shortly to commence studies for his doctorate in the subject. So I suppose one could say that quite a lot has happened since I left Preston in 1951!

In this little book I have let my memories stroll 'down the arches of the years', to quote Preston's own poet Francis Thompson, and I hope my

113

reminiscences have stirred a few happy memories. I have not sought to draw comparisons between Preston then and now. It is up to others to judge which aspects of Preston life are better now, which if any, are not so good, and which things haven't changed. If I were to sum up my time in my home town I would take Preston's unofficial motto 'Proud Preston' and say 'I am Proud to have been a Prestonian'.

My story may have seemed a little autobiographical in places, but I have just told it how I remembered it. I hope my friends whom I have mentioned, and remember with affection, will have delighted with me in recalling their part in my happy childhood; and will have shared a quiet chuckle here and there, with tales of life in Preston half a century or more ago.

My sincere thanks go firstly to Mr Tom Finney CBE JP for so kindly writing the foreword to this book. To Mrs Isabella Walker for her beautiful drawings. To Miss Anna Goddard and the staff of Carnegie Publishing, Preston, for their considerable help and advice. To Vivienne Bennet, Museum and Art Officer and Miss Sally Coleman, Keeper of Social History, the Harris Museum and Art Gallery, Preston; Miss Mena Williams, District Librarian and Mr Shaw, The Harris Library, Preston, for their encouragement and help with research, photographs and maps. To the staff of the District Library Lytham St. Annes. To my dear twin Marjorie and her husband John Margerison for reminding me of facts and events half forgotten; to Barbara 'Babs' Holden for remembering me, and to Harry Cottam for his memories of Deepdale Modern School and photographs of Preston. To Ron Yates for recalling many happy events and good people I knew, and for his photographs; to Mr A. A. Nunn of Cheltenham for his kind comments and for sending me a copy of Sylvia Lovat Corbridge's book 'Its an old Lancashire Custom'; to Mr Albert Evans of New Longton for his picture of Randolph Churchill, for his mementoes of Dances and the Four Aces, and for his reminiscences. To my ever vivacious Cousin Dorothy Satterthwaite (née Blacow) for her helpful contribution and photographs, and just for being herself. To the Trustees of the Imperial War Museum for permission to reproduce Wartime posters. To the editor of the *Lancashire Evening Post* for permission to reproduce photographs, and to Mr Paul Agnew for his help. To Fred Lang for his happy reminders of great times past and for his remarkable influence on my life; to the Reverend Tony Marks for giving me the break I needed, and for his fine little cameo of memories, and finally to my family for proof reading my script, for their very helpful comments, and for not falling about laughing in all the wrong places!